Formative Assessments in a Professional Learning Community

Todd Stanley
Betsy Moore

Eye on Education
6 Depot Way West, Suite 106
Larchmont, NY 10538
(914) 833-0551
(914) 833-0761 fax
www.eyeoneducation.com

Library of Congress Cataloging-in-Publication Data

Stanley, Todd.
Formative assessments in a professional learning community/Todd Stanley and Betsy Moore.
      p.   cm.
ISBN 978-1-59667-167-6
1. Educational tests and measurements—United States. 2. Professional learning communities—United States. I. Moore, Betsy. II. Title.
LB3051.S795 2010
371.26—dc22   2010033504

10 9 8 7 6 5 4 3

Meet the Authors

Todd Stanley began teaching in 1997. A National Board Certified Teacher, he started out in the traditional classroom, teaching junior high students for two years, but quickly was given different growth experiences as a teacher. He taught on a gifted-accelerated team for three years, compacting three years of curriculum into two years of classroom time. He then taught at the Christopher Program, a project-based, integrated curriculum that serviced juniors and seniors, providing many outside learning experiences for students. During this time he also trained teachers from all around the state of Ohio for the Literacy Curriculum Alignment Project (LCAP), helping teachers to align their lessons to state standards and best prepare students for the state achievement tests. Next, Todd created the Ivy Program, a pull-out gifted program for third and fourth graders relying heavily on project-based learning. He currently teaches in the Reynoldsburg School District on the Quest Program, teaching Social Studies and Science to fifth and sixth graders and is the leader of the Critical Friends Group in his school. Todd lives in Pickerington, Ohio with his wife Nicki and his two daughters Anna and Abby.

Betsy Moore is a veteran teacher who retired from Reynoldsburg City Schools after 30 years of service and is currently the Executive Director of *Teacher 2 Teacher* (www .teacher2teacher.info), a national educational consulting company based in Ohio. Betsy began her career as a special education teacher, eventually moving on to the regular education classroom. While in the regular classroom she worked on many cutting-edge strategies including student-led conferences and short-cycle assessments. From 2000–2007 Betsy worked in the Literacy Curriculum Alignment Project (LCAP), training over 1500 teachers in more than 60 schools. She co-authored the book *Short-Cycle Assessment: Improving Student Achievement through Formative Assessment*, which details the process developed in the LCAP work. Betsy co-authored a second book titled *Critical Thinking and Formative Assessments: Raising the Rigor in Your Classroom*, which provides strategies to teach critical thinking skills to all students. In her role with *Teacher 2 Teacher*, Betsy provides quality professional development in the areas of differentiated instruction, vertical alignment, short-cycle assessment development, and developing critical thinking skills, to name a few. Betsy lives with her husband Dave, a retired high school assistant principal, in Columbus, Ohio. She has two grown children: Amy, who lives in Hilliard, Ohio, and Bryan, who lives in Lake Elsinore, California. Also living in Temecula are Betsy's grandchildren Aria Nicole and Micah Rhys.

Table of Contents

Introduction: Why Use Short-Cycle Assessments in a Professional Learning Community?

If schools want to enhance their organizational capacity to boost student learning, they should work on building a professional community that is characterized by shared purpose, collaborative activity, and collective responsibility among staff.

—F. Newmann

This book attempts to answer two very important questions. The first question is, why use short-cycle assessments as formative assessments to improve student achievement? The quick answer is quite simple: because they work. The longer answer involves research and data, some of which has been observed first-hand in the field by the authors of this book. While working with school districts in the state of Ohio we saw remarkable improvements in student success and learning once we transformed schools to a short-cycle assessment model, taking many of them out of continuous school improvement and raising them to an effective rating. Much of this information was researched and documented by Dr. Susan Lang in a study with Miami University titled *An Evaluation Study of Short-Cycle Assessments: An Instructional Process* (Lang, Stanley, & Moore, 2008).

For the record, a short-cycle assessment is a formative assessment, given periodically, and designed to help the teacher shape instruction. What does this look like in practice? A teacher covers a predetermined amount of content, then creates an assessment addressing that content to determine whether students "got it" or not. You're probably thinking this seems like what millions of classrooms already do across the country, but the big difference (and it is a big one) is that most times the instruction of the material ends with the assessment. With a formative assessment, on the other hand, the instruction continues. If there are students who don't "get it," lessons are altered or even retaught. Gaps in teacher, as well as student ability, are exposed and can be addressed, and the direction of the classroom is formed using these assessments.

Formative short-cycle assessments in this process are designed to look exactly like the format of the state test. This way, students, in addition to learning the material, will become familiar with the style of testing the state requires. The benefits of short-cycle assessments extend to both the student and teacher. We call these benefits the "Four Es":

1. **Exposure:** To give students planned and purposeful *exposure* to the standards and formats.
2. **Expertise:** To develop *expertise* in each teacher's ability to ask higher level questions, base instructional decisions for delivery on performance data, and collaborate for curricular direction across grade levels.
3. **Endurance:** To build resilience and *endurance* for each student to be able to a) sit through the test and b) work through difficult questions.
4. **Empower:** To *empower* students and their parents to become responsible decision makers for learning.

The second question this book seeks to answer is, why work in a professional learning community (PLC) to roll out formative short-cycle assessments? The answer is a case of "second verse, same as the first"; because it works. The short-cycle assessment is not designed simply to garner immediate results in a single classroom, although many times this happens. The idea of the short-cycle assessment is to change the culture of the school, so that students are not experiencing the process in a single classroom, but are seeing it throughout their entire school system no matter what grade they are in or teacher they have. Ideally this is not a change but rather a transformation. The school is transforming students and teachers to best prepare for increased student achievement.

DuFour and Eaker (1998), when describing the ideal PLC school include the following:

> At the end of the semester, Connie worked with her teams to analyze the results of student performance on the common comprehensive assessments the teams had developed. . . . They identified areas of concern and then brainstormed steps that they might take to improve the level of student achievement. (p.41)

What this means is using PLCs to create, administer, grade, and analyze the data of the formative assessments. This will lead to schoolwide change if done properly. This book will show step by step how to do this in a PLC.

This book is broken down into nine chapters, each designed to gradually transform a school into a professional learning community that uses formative short-cycle assessments to improve student achievement. Chapter one defines in more detail what a professional learning community is. It also offers descriptions of the different types of PLCs a school can use to work with the formative short-cycle assessment process.

Everyone at one time or another has had a bad experience working in a group. This might be a result of one person being stuck doing all the work, group members not getting along, or any number of other obstacles that prevent groups from producing quality work. Chapter two addresses how to work effectively in groups and how to handle the problems that often crop up.

Once you have been convinced to unfold your formative short-cycle assessments in a PLC, we move into the SCORE Process, chapter three, which is how to develop the actual assessment. Chapter four deals with aligning the curriculum, chapter five outlines the writing of the assessment, and chapter six provides strategies for the giving and grading of the assessment.

The logical question always is—once I have given these assessments, what now? The final three chapters deal with this question. Chapter seven instructs how to analyze the data and make it useful, while chapter eight concerns the adjustments one might make in the classroom based on this data.

Finally, like a good marriage, professional learning communities are not something, which once working properly, will simply sail along smoothly. Group members have to continue working to keep the professional learning community thriving, even when things are going great. This might involve rewriting assessments, fixing problems when they rear their ugly heads, and probably the most neglected aspect, celebrating success. This is why chapter nine is about keeping up with collaboration.

By following the steps outlined in this book you can ensure that your teaching practices will improve as will the achievement of your students. As an extra added bonus, by doing this in your professional learning communities, you will transform the school into a place where collaboration is not just a concept, but a way of life.

1

Why Work in a Professional Learning Community?

> There is growing evidence that the best hope for significant school improvement is transforming schools into professional learning communities.
>
> —Richard DuFour

Surely you have heard the saying, "two heads are better than one." Working within a group offers a lot of advantages—multiple perspectives, someone to watch your back, and a division of labor. Great things can be accomplished in groups, and yet the profession of education is one that typically puts teachers in a place where they work alone. Teachers often find themselves isolated from one another, even when they work on a team. There is occasionally shared planning when teachers can discuss ideas, talk about common students, and figure out scheduling issues, but how much time is devoted to true collaboration and learning? If that time is not deliberate, it often ends up being a meeting regarding incidentals or procedures. There needs to be a place in the educational world for focused collaboration in a professional learning community (PLC).

The irony is that we have our students work in groups, yet when they complain about it, we inform them that they will be required to work in groups their entire lives, making it a valuable skill to learn. But how often as teachers do we work successfully in groups? Like many theories in education, we as teachers have to learn to practice what we preach. The major problem with focused collaboration is that we as teachers are not often properly trained to take advantage of it.

What Is a PLC?

Understanding what a professional learning community is might go a long way in helping to form one. According to Richard DuFour and Robert Eaker in their ground-breaking book, *Professional Learning Communities at Work* (1998), each word was carefully chosen:

Professional: someone who is an expert in a specialized field. All teachers are expected to be professionals including their willingness to improve as educators.

Learning: someone who is not content with the status quo, but is always growing and seeking new opportunities to be a better teacher.

Communities: having the space to create an environment where teachers feel safe and supported in order to "work together to achieve what they cannot accomplish alone". (p. xii)

You put them together and what you get are groups of teachers using their knowledge as educators to try to improve student learning, and overall, the climate of their school. DuFour and Eaker list these characteristics of a PLC (pp. 25–29):

1. Shared mission, vision, and values
2. Collective inquiry
3. Collaborative teams
4. Action oriented and experimentation
5. Continuous improvement
6. Results oriented

This is not just getting together for a meeting or two to enact a temporary mandate. It is about seeking school change, even if that means doing it one classroom at a time. To create a PLC the focus needs to be on learning rather than teaching, working collaboratively with others, and most important, holding all members accountable for results.

Advantages to Working in a PLC

The advantages to working in a PLC are many. First and foremost it puts teachers together in the room in order to collaborate with one another. How often does that happen in today's educational world? By working together, teachers can create wonderful things that would not be possible working alone. Even Thomas Edison worked with a team of inventors in order to develop his many brilliant ideas.

Some would argue it is easier to do things alone, that too many people offering ideas is like too many cooks in the kitchen, but this is not the case if every cook has a specific role. Walk into any great restaurant in the world and you will find many cooks in the kitchen, all doing something different, with the end result being a wonderful meal. If just one cook had to produce this meal for a multitude of people, he would get bogged down in the work, and it would take forever to receive your food. All the cooks working together, however, are able to produce a medley of fine-tasting food.

Similarly, a multitude of teachers can create a better learning environment for their school than can a single teacher.

Here are some of the advantages to working in a PLC:

- ◆ Sharing ideas
- ◆ Working to close achievement gaps
- ◆ Getting everyone on the same page
- ◆ Dividing up the work
- ◆ Making change more widespread
- ◆ Creating community

Any one of these advantages would be a good reason to work in a PLC, but the fact that all of these put together combine to improve student learning makes for a compelling argument.

Disadvantages to Working in a PLC

It would be nice if there were not any disadvantages to working in a PLC, but they do exist under certain circumstances. Here are some of them:

- ◆ Requires more time to get tasks done in a group
- ◆ Not having available time in the school day to meet
- ◆ Getting people to agree with each other
- ◆ Lack of support from administration
- ◆ Working with people who don't buy into the plan
- ◆ Working with people who are afraid of change

Most of these disadvantages are perceptions. Being afraid of change or thinking people won't agree with one another can be solved with a lot of support and education regarding the process. Other disadvantages, such as time concerns, can be solved with a little bit of organization. There is no doubt that support from central office and administration can go a long way in greasing the skids for the PLC process concerning formative assessment.

Different Types of PLCs

How you organize your PLC is dependent upon your needs. The alignment will look much different if you are trying to implement formative assessments as a department, a grade level, or a school. There is no right or wrong in regard to these set-ups, but there are ones that offer greater advantages than others.

Here are some examples of professional learning communities:

- Team
- Content area
- Grade level
- School
- District
- Multiple districts

One of the easiest ways to roll out formative assessments is on a *team* of teachers. For instance, if you have four teachers who work with the same group of students, you could develop formative short-cycle assessments together. This is easier because of the management aspect; it is simpler to coordinate and organize four people than it is 40. It is also easier to get four people to come to an agreement than a room full of people. This is the type of PLC that works well within an elementary or a middle school setting when teachers have the students for all subject areas, or departmentalize while keeping the students together in a core group.

Rolling out the formative assessment process as a team rather than as individual teachers is better because the pool of students become accustomed to taking formative assessments in every classroom. Many times when students have four different teachers, they are dealing with four very distinctive styles and sets of expectations. By the teachers working together and having a common set of expectations, the students do not have to switch gears and are more comfortable as a result.

What this type of PLC typically looks like are the teachers sitting down and agreeing on the specifics of the formative short-cycle assessment process beginning with the format of the questions, for example, short answer, multiple choice, response grids, or written prompts. Usually the format is determined by modeling the state assessment. Teachers should also agree to the number of questions and how the assessments will be administered. The assessments themselves are typically written by the individual teacher based on his or her expertise on the subject, but the science teacher might offer some helpful criticism for the math assessment, or the English teacher might have some things to say about proper grammar on the Social Studies assessment, and so on.

Since the advantage of similar format and expectations becomes even more pronounced as the number in the group increases, the one true disadvantage in working in a team such as this is it affects only a limited number of teachers instead of transforming the culture of the school.

Another option to work in a PLC is as a *content area*, which is a bit more complicated, but offers many advantages as well. This would involve two or three English teachers, or all five science teachers in a given grade, deciding to give a common formative short-cycle assessment. Since the grade level of the individual student taking the course may vary in a high school, this is the type of PLC that may work best in that setting. Here the teachers will be sharing the content being taught where in the elementary/middle school setting they are sharing the students.

The following is an example of what this type of PLC might look like. There are four teachers that teach Algebra. The four of them decide what they will be teaching within the course of a given period. Although they might not be teaching the same content on exactly the same day, all four teachers are charged with teaching certain standards within a timeframe, typically a grading period. At the end of the grading period, all Algebra students would take a common assessment with questions covering the agreed upon standards, written by the four teachers.

One advantage of working in this type of group is it maintains a balance of content. Even when teachers are using the same textbook, there are some teachers that value some standards more than others. If you have a teacher whose undergraduate focus was in statistics, he might find himself placing a larger amount of class time to this content because it is something he is very comfortable with. You may have another teacher who does not see much value in teaching measurement and so moves through these skills quite quickly, covering them but not going into any depth. This is not done maliciously or to try and deny students certain content, but we all have our strengths and weaknesses as teachers and often play to our strengths. By having to decide as a group which standards to cover, more than likely everything is given its just due and content is not being missed.

The other thing working in this type of PLC does is to allow these four Algebra teachers the opportunity to share ideas about what works in their classrooms. For example, the group might discover that one class is really getting the number sense questions, while another is struggling. Those teachers can share what is being done in their classroom and hopefully this will serve to improve instruction in the classroom.

The disadvantage to working in a grade level PLC is finding time for the teachers to get together for these conversations. It is unlikely all the teachers in a given content at a grade level have a common planning time so time needs to be carved out for them at the beginning or end of the day. In an environment where there are many different meetings and interruptions including the continual volley of announcements over the PA, this can be a challenge.

Increasing the involvement of staff members in a PLC is something that would begin to transform the culture of the school. Formative assessments can also be implemented within an entire *grade level*. This type of PLC involves all teachers in a particular grade working together to create, administer, grade, and analyze the formative short-cycle assessments. In this case several subject areas get together and create a common pacing chart and set of common assessments.

An example of what this would look like in a school is a group of third grade teachers getting together to create common assessments for all four state tested subject areas. If the state only tests in language arts and math as many do, the group may choose to only involve those two subject areas. The end result is the same however; a common set of assessments that every student in the third grade takes.

The advantages of a grade level PLC are the same advantages as those mentioned for the content area PLC, except even more ideas can be shared and even more people will be on the same page making sure the proper content is instructed. The disadvantages to this type of PLC are also the same, only perhaps even more difficult to manage. How do you find time for an entire grade level to work together? There has to be some effort by a standards coordinator or building administrator to provide this common time to create and implement the formative assessment process.

If you take this theory of grade level PLCs and multiple it by however many grades you have in a given school, you could have an entire *school* creating and administering common formative short-cycle assessments. How this looks is a junior high consisting of grades 6 through 8 who create short-cycle assessments for common classes. That means all the 6th-grade language arts students will take a common assessment at the end of the 9 week grading period. The 8th-grade biology classes will do the same thing, and so on.

The advantage here is that the 6th grader who becomes familiar with taking short-cycle assessments, knows she will encounter it in her 7th- and 8th-grade year as well, exposing her to the format of the short-cycle assessment and preparing her even more for the year-end state tests. All the students at this school will be familiar with the system of assessment and know what the expectations are.

This can be taken one step further if you consider the use of formative short-cycle assessments throughout the entire *district* in all of its schools. In our experience working with over 20 school districts, the ones that met with the most success were those who worked as a district to enact the formative short-cycle assessment process. Their success had nothing to do with the student population, but everything to do with working together as a staff, from administration to resource teachers. The districts that seemed to encounter the most difficulty were those that did not approach this change as a community. A couple of teachers were very enthusiastic, but did not get the proper support from other teachers or from administration and eventually became frustrated with the process.

The reason such an approach is ideal for PLCs and formative assessment is because it is easier to change the entire culture when the majority of the staff is on board. For students it simply becomes a way of life as they realize it does not matter the content area or grade level—they will encounter short-cycle assessments in all of their classes.

An even larger task would be to implement a formative short-cycle assessment process across *multiple districts*. On one occasion we worked with most of the schools in a given county, bringing teachers from several school districts together to create common formative assessments. Another situation had us coordinating nine districts across two counties. Although this takes an immense amount of coordination, it can be done to great success. There has to be support at several levels and someone willing to facilitate the communication among so many schools, such as an instructional coach. The major advantage to this is the increased level of collaboration with teachers who would have never had the opportunity to work with another in a large PLC, sharing ideas.

The other major advantage for the districts we worked with involved the many students who moved from school to school and district to district. Students with great mobility typically repeat or miss content. For example, a student in district A may have been learning life science the first 6 weeks of school and getting ready to learn earth science. The student then moves to district B where they are getting ready to learn life science and have already done earth science. The mobile student is now going to be taught life science twice and earth science not at all, creating a gap. In the districts working together, on the other hand, everyone in the county was on the same page, and students moving from district to district were not losing anything in the process.

Finding the type of PLC that works best for you is something that needs to be agreed upon. The more people who get involved the greater the possible advantages, but at the same time introducing PLCs to a large group who are not ready for buy-in can cause the efforts to fail. Sometimes introducing PLCs to a small group and showing others its success can be the route to take. To determine which of these PLCs might be best for you and help give you a big picture outlook, consult the *Advantages/Disadvantages of PLC Groups* chart on page 95 of the Blueprints section in the back of this book.

If You Learn One Thing From This Chapter . . .

Professional learning communities are a great way to transform a school, allowing teachers the chance to collaborate with one another and providing students with consistency. Whereas there are both advantages and disadvantages to using PLCs, many times the disadvantages can be avoided with clear communication and/or good organization. The type of PLC you decide to use depends upon how many people are willing or open to such an endeavor. Know that the more people you can get on board, the larger the transformation will be for your school.

2

How to Work Effectively in a Group

The productivity of a work group seems to depend on how the group members see their own goals in relation to the goals of the organization.

—Ken Blanchard

Working effectively in a group is essential when forming a professional learning community. Sometimes this process is easygoing because the people involved are all working toward the same goal. The larger the group gets however, the more difficult it is to reach harmony. That is why it is important to establish a positive group environment where everyone is rowing their oars in the same direction instead of paddling against one another.

Here are some characteristics of a good group environment:

♦ Each member is willing to contribute.
♦ There is a relaxed climate for communication.
♦ All members develop a mutual trust.
♦ The group and individuals are prepared to take risks.
♦ The group is clear about goals and establishes targets.
♦ Member roles are defined.
♦ Members know how to examine errors without personal attacks.
♦ The group has capacity to create new ideas.
♦ Each member knows he can influence the agenda.

The question becomes how do you get to this point? How are the climate and trust established, especially with groups of people who have never worked together before or, even worse, have worked together and have a history of difficulty? Let's examine this question.

Creating a Good Group Environment Using Norms

It is important to establish a good group environment. One way to do this fairly easily is to establish *norms*, which are agreements suggested by the group and that have been approved by everyone. They are different from rules because rules are meant to catch people doing something wrong; norms are just the way things are—the expectations so to speak. It is very important that these norms are not handed down from administrators or decreed by a curriculum coordinator, but instead are created by the people directly involved in the group.

A specific process should be used when creating group norms. Begin by asking the question, "What does this group need in order to be effective?" It could be the physical environment such as a place to meet without interruption, or a mental environment such as a place people feel emotionally safe. For some groups this conversation will come quite naturally; for others, a space may need to be created to allow ideas to be shared.

Start the process by having members write their suggestions on sticky notes. Once you have given people a few minutes to jot down ideas, have them cluster the notes according to similarities. Grouping like ideas on a whiteboard or chart paper is one way to accomplish this. It will become clear that some ideas have several sticky notes while some stand alone. The clusters should then be read to the whole group who will use these suggestions to craft a specific norm (for a step-by-step script for forming norms, check out *Forming Norms*, p. 96 in the Blueprints section). If a group has difficulty sharing or has a mix of dominating personalities, an impartial participant may be needed to help moderate setting the norms. This allows any group bias to be eliminated and allows everyone to feel as though things were done in a fair and impartial manner.

The reason group norms are so effective is because they are created by those involved in the group. If someone has a problem with a suggestion, it does not become a norm, or it is altered to be more accommodating. For instance, suppose someone suggests there be no cell phones at meetings because they cause a distraction. A different member of the group may have a young child at home and needs to be reachable as a result. The compromise may be that cell phones have to be turned to vibrate so they don't distract as much.

Here are some typical group norms:

- ◆ Start and end each meeting on time
- ◆ Allow the opportunity for everyone to speak freely
- ◆ Provide food/snacks for each meeting
- ◆ Do not put down other's ideas
- ◆ Must be able to laugh
- ◆ Seek solutions rather than complain
- ◆ Leave the room to take a cell phone call
- ◆ Set an agenda for the next meeting before leaving the current one

These are merely suggestions to provide a jumping off point. Each group must create its own norms in order to feel ownership. It is important to note that group norms are not written in stone. They should always remain in draft form so that new ones can be added if a problem arises while others may be jettisoned because of lack of clarity or compliance. We once had a group where certain individuals could never get to the meeting on time even though we had it as one of our norms. Rather than let it cause resentment and derision among the group, we simply chose to strike it from the norms. This way members felt alright with coming late and this simply became an accepted practice. It is interesting that fewer people came late to meetings after we dropped this norm.

It is important that group norms are visible at every meeting, either through copies everyone has in front of them or displayed in the room. At the beginning of every meeting group norms should be read aloud. The norms are only effective if the group is mindful of them. The minute the norms slide into the background, they will be forgotten and inevitably violated more and more often.

There needs to be a procedure to follow if someone is violating one of the norms. For instance, rather than calling that person out individually, the group may simply want to revisit the norm. Is it something the group is willing to commit to, or does it need to be changed? By handling this as a group, no one is embarrassed and the person is reminded of his responsibility to the group. This will ideally alter the behavior as a result. If the behavior persists, it might be necessary for the group to address the person individually under the spirit of open and honest conversation that most groups establish as a norm.

All Work and No Play Makes Jack a Dull Boy

The same can be said for PLCs. If work is all that is ever done in them, members may begin to resist them. There has to be time built in to loosen things up and have some occasional fun. One way this can happen is by having a social time worked into the agenda. People, especially teachers, are social animals by nature; they want to get together and share stories about students with others whom they may not get a chance to talk to very often. Building in this social time eliminates the temptation to digress from the work items on the agenda. If 5 to 10 minutes of social time to chat at the beginning is built in, it might give the group a more focused and effective 50 minutes than if the entire hour was devoted to working. It is important to not let this 5 to 10 minutes turn into 15 to 20 minutes, lest the rare shared time get away. It is also important to make the group aware that this time has been designated so that those who are not as social don't think their time is being wasted. That type of frustration can lead to resentment.

Sometimes this social time comes quite naturally to a group; other times it might be necessary to create activities for them, especially if this is a group of members who do not know each other well or have not had the opportunity to work with one another. These activities are designed to allow the group to get more comfortable with one another before getting down to the serious business of work. They are called icebreakers and help set a relaxed tone.

A simple icebreaker to get a read on who you are dealing with that day is to ask each of the group members if they were _____, what would they be and why? For instance, if you were an ice cream flavor, what would you be? Explain your rationale for the choice.

Possible answers you might hear:

- Neapolitan, because I have to be a lot of different things to a lot of different people.
- Vanilla, because I appeal to everyone.
- Rocky Road because the kids have been awful today.
- Pralines and Cream, because I'm a little nuts.

With this icebreaker, anything could be substituted for ice cream: color, animal, sport, flower, or music. We once asked a roomful of 35 teachers what car they would be. We were amazed as we went around the room, how every teacher mentioned a different type of car. Some of them were fairly clever, such as the special education teacher who said she was the short bus, or the teacher who was having an especially bad week and said she was the junker being dragged behind by the tow truck. Such an activity usually gets people laughing and reveals a little bit about each person. If someone indicates she is having a bad day, the group will know they should tread lightly with her, while if someone is particularly positive, she may spread her feelings among the group.

Icebreakers shouldn't take more than a few minutes. The benefit to icebreakers is they will allow the meeting to take an informal tone while encouraging people to relax a little. There are more icebreaker activities on pages 97 and 98, *Ice Breaker Activities* and *Icebreaker Bingo*.

Group Building Activities

When starting out with a new group it is important to know the dynamics. One thing that causes more trouble in groups than anything else is working with a person who has a different style than the rest of the group. Because her methods are often misunderstood, she may be interpreted as difficult, not different. For instance, if someone is a fast worker and someone else is slow, the fast working person might think the slower person is holding the group back. From the slower worker's perspective, however, she just needs time to process and understand. Her perception of the person who works at a faster pace may be that by going so fast, rash decisions are being made. Such a difference can cause tension and splinter group dynamics. If, however, each member knows and understands the differences between them, they are much easier to accept.

Various activities can identify the range of learning styles and differences within a group. One activity that is fairly easy to do yet effective is the *Compass Points* activity (pp. 99–100 in the Blueprints section), which is based on the premise that everyone identifies with one of the compass points that describe work personalities. For instance, someone who is an action person, likes to get things done quickly, and hates it when people slow down the process would be considered a "North." A person who likes to consider everyone's feelings, needs to be sure everyone is on board before moving forward, and is generally an empathetic person would be labeled a "South." A very detailed person, one who likes structure, and is known for being organized, would be considered a "West." A big picture thinker; someone who analyzes everything, almost to the point of bringing everything to a screeching halt, is an "East."

There are obviously some directions that work better with others. West and East tend to do well together because while one is analyzing, the other has the chance to get the details. A South typically gets along with anyone because this person is nervous about offending someone and constantly tries to please everyone. A person who is a North, while getting things done, can tend to neglect the needs of the other three directions. Some people may have characteristics of more than one direction and would be considered an intermediate direction—in other words they might be someone who is detailed and empathetic toward others, making them a Southwest. Or they might be a big picture person who still likes to get things done, putting them at Northeast.

To begin this activity the facilitator of the group would read the descriptions of the various directions and have people stand around the room in the group that best describes them.

The four directions are labeled in Figure 2.1. The person who is an intermediate direction such as Southeast would be asked to choose the cardinal direction with which she most identifies. Once groups have formed, the members will, as a group, reflect on four things:

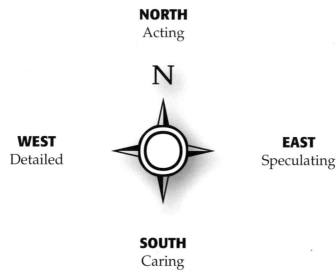

NORTH
Acting

WEST
Detailed

EAST
Speculating

SOUTH
Caring

FIGURE 2.1 Compass Points

1. What adjectives would describe strengths from your compass direction?
2. What adjectives would describe weaknesses from your compass direction?
3. Which compass direction do you think you would work best with? Which would be the most challenging?
4. If your team did not have your compass direction, how do you think it would function?

Responses may be recorded on chart paper or a piece of notebook paper. After about 5 minutes of reflection (the west will never get done because they will get bogged down in the details while the north will be finished in 3 minutes), the groups should report their reflections. Someone should record the reflections in case further review is necessary.

This activity accomplishes a couple of things. Right off the bat it lets people know that different personality types reside within the group. It is important to understand that not everyone works in the same way. Physically seeing this can go a long way in helping others tolerate differences. It also gives each direction hints on how to work with one another. A North can come to understand if they just listen a little longer, working with the west will be that much easier. Last, this activity makes people realize that without the other directions it would be difficult to function successfully as a group. A group of all East members might have ground-breaking discussions on educational practices, but without the West to organize the findings, they wouldn't do anything but talk. The North might get things done in record time, but without the West there to slow them down a little, it might not be the best quality. The South people will wait until everyone is on board, not able to move forward without a north to push them. Ideally, for best results in a group, people from all directions are necessary.

Another good activity for group building is the *Profile of a Student* developed by Gene Thompson-Grove for the National School Reform Faculty (2008). In this activity, participants identify with one of nine different student profiles read from descriptions on pages 101–102 of the Blueprints section. Following this, strategies for working with the type of students are discussed and shared with the group. This is similar to the compass points activity except more choices are available, and it is sometimes easier for people to identify themselves. This is also a good activity to do in the classroom with students so it has professional development benefits as well.

The reason we have chosen these two examples is because they are activities that can be done with four people or forty. There are many other group building activities that are available. *Group Building Activities*, pages 103–104 of the Blueprints section describes more activities.

Cancer in the Clubhouse

Possibly there will come a time and place where you will have someone in your group that causes a rift in your group dynamics. This may be because the person always thinks negatively, it could be because the person is lazy and does not want to do anything, or it could be because the person is ambivalent of the process and refuses to help. Whatever the reason, it is important that, just like real cancer, this disease is caught in its early stages before it has a chance to spread. If you ignore this problem and hope it goes away, it won't. And as it spreads it will pull more people in until it isn't just one person, but several people who are disgruntled in the PLC.

The question becomes how should this situation be handled? Because the group is made up of adults, you would hope the disgruntled person would figure things out and act accordingly. Unfortunately, many times this is not the case. At the same time, this person is a professional colleague and should be treated with the same respect you would afford to all members. Just because one person is acting unprofessionally does not mean other members of the group should as well.

You may sense that the person is being uncooperative because he does not agree with the process. We have found that most people who are resistant to formative short-cycle assessments feel that way for one of three reasons: a) ignorance, b) fear, or c) they don't see the value of the process. Let's examine these one at a time.

When people do not understand something, most times their first reaction is to label the process as "stupid." In the case of short-cycle assessments, people think it is "teaching to the test," as though this is a bad idea. It is important to educate these people. This may come in a reading of an article by the group, or an expert explaining it, or maybe even a one-on-one conversation.

A second possibility is that the person is afraid. Many times people are fearful of change simply because it is different. If someone has been doing something for years that in her mind is working and is all of a sudden told to do something else, she may feel that this devalues her hard work. Finding a way to honor past work, either by providing a space for her to share, or by allowing her a venue for productive venting may help to circumvent the fear. The more people bottle things up, the more dangerous it becomes when their frustration or fear finally blows.

People also might not like being held accountable. The short-cycle assessment process most certainly holds teachers accountable, but to themselves, not in a way that will be used against them come contract time. If a principal is using these results as a staff evaluation, the teachers will never trust the process. Teachers need to know they are in a safe place to make mistakes and grow as educators.

Third, we often run across teachers who do not see the value in the formative short-cycle assessment process. They resent having teaching time taken away or feel the state tests students to death. They have seen educational movements come and go as they often do and figure if they wait it out, this one will go by the wayside as well. Unfortunately times are changing and high-stakes testing is only going to get larger before it gets smaller. The sobering question to ask a teacher feeling this way is, what is best for kids? Since students will have to take the high-stakes tests, isn't it in their best interest to be prepared? The entire goal of every teacher from kindergarten all the way to seniors is seeing a student graduate from high school. In order to do that in most states, students have to pass a state-mandated assessment. These formative short-cycle assessments are designed to help do that very thing.

Sometimes when simple explanations and education of short-cycle assessment work is not enough to overcome the obstacles, the group must be patient and let the process speak for itself. There were some individuals with whom we worked who suddenly saw the value in the formative short-cycle assessment process after working with it for a number of years. Only time allowed the light bulb to go on. The important thing is for the group to try and figure out where the disgruntled person is coming from and meet the person there. This is the only way the group will become productive.

Sometimes, too, there is that rare individual who simply wants nothing to do with the process. If there are enough people on board who do believe in the process, this person can be isolated and won't do any damage to the group dynamics. Awareness and patience is critical when dealing with a cancer in the clubhouse.

Good Meetings vs. Bad Meetings

One thing that can go a long way in creating a good group environment is running effective meetings. Teachers do not like to feel as though their time is wasted; time is one of the few precious commodities we have as educators. Having group members motivated to do work sometimes comes down to having effective meetings so they feel valued. Although a lot of things can go wrong at a meeting, from arguments to constant interruptions, there are some things that can, and should, be controlled as much as possible. Here is a top-five list of good vs. bad meetings:

1. Good meetings start and end on time. Bad meetings start or end late, throwing everything else off.
2. Good meetings almost always have an agenda. Bad meetings have no focus and thus nothing gets accomplished.
3. Good meetings allow people to collaborate with one another. Bad meetings isolate people into working by themselves or involve people being talked at.
4. Good meetings give people the right amount of space to do what they need to. Bad meetings are in a place not conducive to what the group is doing (such as, too small, not the proper lighting or equipment, poor room temperature).
5. Good meetings accomplish something. Bad meetings just result in more meetings.

In the end, knowing whether you are conducting good or bad meetings comes down to the following: People want to attend a good meeting; people can't wait to get out of a bad one.

If You Learn One Thing From This Chapter . . .

In order to have an effective group environment, the tone must be set early on. It is like making a first impression; you have only a single chance to do this. If you start off a PLC on the wrong foot, you might lose the ability of the group to work effectively toward the same goal. Using activities such as setting norms, icebreakers, and identifying team learning styles like compass points will help set the right environment. Controlling what you can in meetings, such as physical space and other organizational things, and making sure to address possible threats to the group dynamics, such as negative people or those who do not understand the process, will help improve the efficiency of the PLC.

3

Starting the SCORE Process

Nothing is particularly hard if you divide it into small jobs.

—Henry Ford

Although creating formative, short-cycle assessments for an entire school or school district might seem like an overwhelming task, dividing it into small jobs makes it much easier. That is why we have divided the short-cycle assessment process into eight parts, all which fit together to create formative assessments that could change the culture of your school.

This process is called the SCORE Process. SCORE stands for:

S—Short
C—Cycle assessments
O—Organized for
R—Results and
E—Expectations

Figure 3.1 illustrates the SCORE Process and its eight steps. None of these steps is particularly difficult when divided up among your professional learning community. Take it one step at a time for a fairly smooth process. This chapter will cover Steps 1 and 2 of the SCORE Process.

What Does Everyone Know?

The first two steps of the SCORE Process involve the understanding of the state standards and the state assessment. It is important to figure out the level of expertise of each of the members within the PLC. Do some people successfully integrate the state standards into their classroom curriculum already, while others do not adhere to the standards at all? With the adoption of the Common Core Standards, are teachers fully aware of how the standards will change and how those changes will affect instruction? Are there people who are aware there is a state assessment but that is about all they know, compared with people who may have sat on the committee that helped

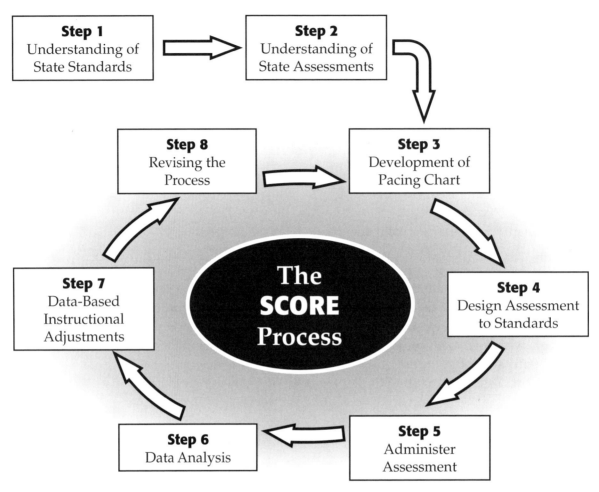

FIGURE 3.1 The SCORE Process

write the state assessment? Figuring out the level of expertise in a PLC is similar to finding out what students know in a classroom. You don't want to waste time reviewing something everyone already knows, but at the same time you don't want to assume and not teach something they need.

One way to avoid guessing about the knowledge level of the PLC is to begin with an activity called a "consensogram." In this activity a question is placed on a piece of chart paper and participants rate themselves in terms of their understanding and expertise. There can be as many pieces of chart paper as there are questions. Examples of questions that will lead to knowing the level of expertise with regard to the first step in the SCORE Process might be:

- ◆ How comfortable are you with the state standards?
- ◆ How often do you mention the state standards in your classroom?
- ◆ How confident would you be teaching other teachers about the state standards?

- If your state is adopting the Common Core Standards, how knowledgeable are you about them?
- Are you confident that you can easily incorporate the new Common Core Standards in your curriculum at both the instructional and the assessment levels?
- How familiar are you with the format (types of questions) on the state assessment?
- How familiar are you with the content (standards covered) by the state assessment?
- Will the state assessment change after the Common Core Standards are adopted? If yes, do you know what those changes will be?

Group members are given dot stickers and asked to place one dot per question on a scale from 1 to 5. Placing the dot above the 1 means nothing is known about the topic, while placing a dot above the 5 means the group member has expert knowledge. Placement of the dot stickers on the chart should be in a column format—equivalent to what a bar graph would look like. For instance if someone puts their sticker on a 4, and another person also wants to place it on the 4, he would put the sticker right above the other, creating a column. Following the completion of all of the graphs, it will be evident how comfortable the group is with the topic addressed by each question. Figure 3.2 illustrates what a consensogram might look like.

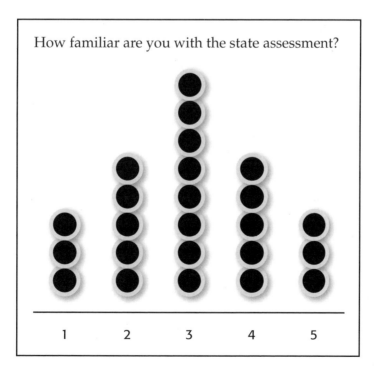

FIGURE 3.2 Consensogram

This exercise will allow the group to get a good idea where everyone is, or at least where they think they are. If the consensogram shows there is a lot of inexperience, you might consider spending a lot of time on the academic standards. This may be necessary as the Common Core Standards come into adoption. Likewise, if the consensogram shows a lot of experience, the process can begin at a later point. The group has essentially been pre-tested to create a lesson to meet them where they are, much like effective teachers do with classroom students.

A consensogram not only determines where individual group members fall with regard to a topic, it also shows members where they are as a group. If the SCORE Process was automatically started at the beginning, someone (probably a north) who has some experience might resent the slow start. If, however, she sees that most of the other people in the room are starting out raw, starting at the beginning makes more sense to her and will likely result in greater patience and a leadership role using her expertise.

Understanding the Standards

Step one of the SCORE Process is becoming familiar with the state standards. (See Figure 3.3.) Depending on where the group is according to the concensogram determines how deep you will approach the first couple of steps in the SCORE Process. If there are a lot of inexperienced people, especially in regard to the new Common Core Standards, it may be helpful to print out the standards, make copies for everyone, and go over them one by one as a group. Discussion should center around what the standards mean to everyone, whether everyone understands what the standard is asking of students, and what knowledge needs to be covered in order for students to get it. This is a good time for collaboration to occur as teachers study the standards and become familiar with them. It is at this time teachers might share lessons used in the past to teach skills and concepts related to the standards. These conversations are extremely valuable as others can pick up ideas.

If there is a high level of familiarity within your PLC, you might want to briefly discuss some of the more difficult standards, talking about the problems in teaching them or the difficulty students have in understanding them. Once again, this is a great opportunity for collaboration. Teachers can share ideas they have used in the classroom to teach the more challenging standards.

One word of caution when you get a group of teachers together to talk—it may become like that scene in the movie *Jaws* where Richard Dreyfuss and Robert Shaw are comparing their shark scars, trying to trump the other. We find that teachers love to tell stories, and it is important to let them do this, but be careful it doesn't digress into a big complaining session about students or the system, trying to one-up each other in war stories. The group facilitator might have to right the ship from time to time and keep the PLC focused on the task at hand which is why norms, an agenda, and a well-planned meeting are essential to the success of the process.

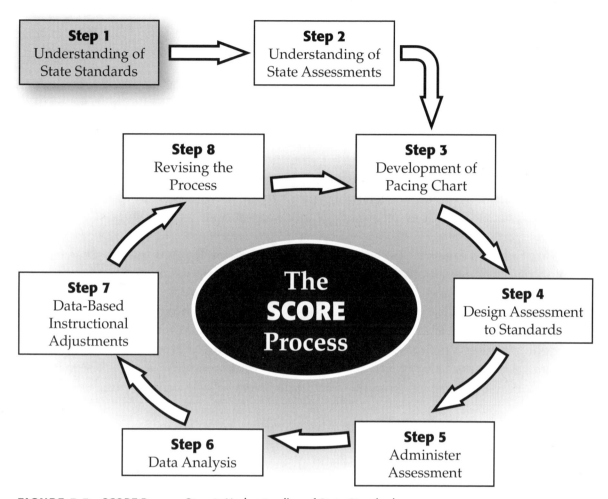

FIGURE 3.3 SCORE Process-Step 1: Understanding of State Standards

Identifying the Level of the Standards
According to Bloom's Taxonomy

As group members become familiar with the standards, it is important to identify at what level of Bloom's Taxonomy each standard is written. This will be an indicator of the level of the questions the state will ask on the high-stakes assessment. In addition, this will inform teachers where they need to begin instruction according to the level of Bloom's Taxonomy. One of the additional questions you can ask in your consensogram may concern the PLCs knowledge of Bloom's Taxonomy. For the record, here are the various levels and their definitions as based on Bloom's Taxonomy, developed by Linda G. Barton, M.S.Ed., 1997:

1. *Knowledge:* exhibit memory of previously learned material by recalling facts, terms, basic concepts, and answers.

2. *Comprehension:* demonstrate understanding of facts and ideas by organizing, comparing, translating, interpreting, giving descriptions, and stating main ideas.
3. *Application:* solve problems to new situations by applying acquired knowledge, facts, techniques, and rules in a different way
4. *Analysis:* examine and break information into parts by identifying motives or causes; make inferences and find evidence to support generalizations.
5. *Synthesis:* compile information together in a different way by combining elements in a new pattern or proposing alternative solutions.
6. *Evaluation:* present and defend opinions by making judgments about information, validity of ideas, or quality of work based on a set of criteria.

These are tiered in the order of the level of thinking. Knowledge is the most basic level, simple recall, while evaluation is the highest level, having to create judgments on ideas based on knowledge and other criteria.

As a PLC, you will want to examine each standard and make a decision about the level of Bloom's at which the students are asked to perform. One way to do this is to first identify the verb being used in the standard. This verb can often indicate the level of Bloom's. See *Bloom's Key Words* chart in the Blueprints section, page 105. For instance, take the following standard from the 5th Grade Science California Content Standards:

Identify the dependent and controlled variables in an investigation.

In this case, the verb is *identify*. Typically this would indicate this standard is at the level of knowledge—the students simply have to memorize dependent and controlled variables and point them out upon seeing them. This is an easy example, but other times the standards are much more challenging and the level is not so obvious. Here is another standard, this time from the 3rd Grade Math Texas Essential Knowledge and skills:

Compare fractional parts of whole objects or sets of objects in a problem situation using concrete models.

In this example, the verb is *compare*, which could fit in one of two categories: comprehension or analysis. The question becomes, which? To determine this the context in which the word is used needs to be examined. Because this standard deals with putting parts together, by definition this would be an analysis. This is where working in a PLC group is very helpful because many experts are at hand, and discussion and debate surrounding the standard can occur. Achieving a consensus about the level of the standard will help everyone to understand the level at which the standard should be instructed and assessed.

Sometimes a standard will have two levels in it, such as this 10th Grade Reading New York performance indicator:

Distinguish between different forms of poetry, such as sonnet, lyric, elegy, narrative, epic, and ode, and recognize how the author uses poetic form to convey message or intent.

The highest level should be used when assigning a level to the standard. *Distinguish* is a comprehension level, while *recognize* is knowledge, so the standard will need to be categorized at the higher level of Bloom's—comprehension.

This labeling of each standard and its level of Bloom's is something we call coding. To organize these codes, you can use the blank *Taxonomy Table* on p. 106) in the Blueprints section.The standard headings are written in the left-hand column and identification of each part of the (sometimes called "performance objectives") are made according to the six levels of Bloom's, which are found in the top row of the table. Figure 3.4 is an example of a completed Taxonomy Table for Social Studies. Shown here are the various numbered strands of History broken down by the level of Bloom's, followed by People in Societies, Geography, and so on. Some states number these strands while others do not. You will need to decide within the PLC how to identify the standards so it makes sense on the Taxonomy Table. Coding these standards within your PLC early on will make things easier for the work down the road.

Social Studies

	Knowledge	Comprehension	Application	Analysis	Synthesis	Evaluate
History	1	5	2, 4	3		
People in Societies		2, 3	1	4		
Geography	1, 2, 3, 6		5			4
Government			1	4, 5	2	3
Citizenship	3, 4	1	5	2	6	7, 8
Economics		6	1, 2, 3, 4		5	

FIGURE 3.4 Taxonomy Table

A clear understanding of these standards is an important stepping stone in the formative short-cycle assessment process. It is essentially the foundation of the process and without it the rest of the work will be built on shaky ground. Making sure there is a solid foundation of the understanding of the standards within the PLC is imperative to the success of the work of the group.

Understanding the State Assessment

Step 2 in the SCORE Process is an understanding of the state test. (See Figure 3.5.) As is the case with Step 1 of the SCORE Process, if there is unfamiliarity with Step 2 within the PLC, some groundwork may need to be done. Printing up copies of past assessments (the department of education website for your state usually will post these) and then analyzing these tests as a group will help develop understanding as to what types of questions are asked, which standards are being addressed by the questions, and

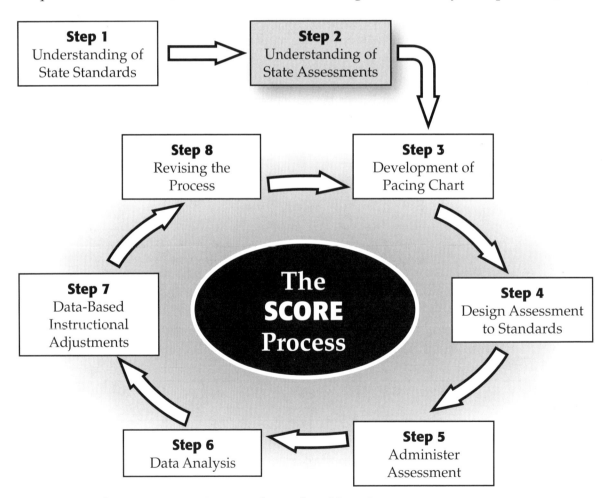

FIGURE 3.5 The SCORE Process-Step 2: Understanding of State Assessments

what patterns may exist. Teachers will want to look at the state test concerning their subject areas. By analyzing these assessments, teachers will begin to understand what the state expects and be able to convey this to their students to help them be prepared.

If there is already a high understanding of the state assessment within the PLC, then groups may want to start with some data analysis of past assessments. Teachers could go through some of the assessment questions students have had difficulty with according to the data provided by the state. As a group, try to pinpoint what might have caused this difficulty, whether it be a poorly worded question, an easy misunderstanding, or a standard not covered as well as it could have been. This type of examination still requires analyzing the test, only at a higher level than a group going through seeking basic understanding. This differentiation of levels is important so people see the value in the SCORE Process immediately and are not turned off by being asked to spend time on something they already know.

Coding the Test

One activity worth considering when working in Step 2 of the SCORE Process is coding the test. This involves going through past state assessments, question by question, and determining which standard the question is specifically addressing (you can keep a running tally on how many times a specific standard is addressed using the blank *Tally Sheet for Standards and the State Assessment* in the Blueprints section, page 107). Going over 2 or 3 years' worth of tests will show a clear pattern of standards most used. Sometimes a standard will be repeated several times on the test, others will appear one year and not another, while some may never appear on any of the tests.

This is important to know and understand because it affects the way teachers instruct. As teachers and experts in our subject area, we like to think we know what is important and what is not, but this is often based on personal opinion. There are some English teachers who feel spelling is a very valuable skill and spend much class time having students study and take spelling quizzes. There are others who feel this memorization is not necessary and that a more valuable skill that serves the same purpose is knowing how to successfully maneuver oneself through a dictionary. Neither one is right nor wrong, they are merely different skills that solve the same problem of knowing how to spell.

The issue becomes what does the state focus on in its year-end assessment? If the state test has a heavy emphasis on spelling but not dictionary skills, then that might alter the approach the teacher takes, or conversely, if the state assessment has a lot of dictionary skills and nothing on spelling, a change in the classroom practice in some classrooms might be necessary.

As a result of No Child Left Behind Act 2002 (NCLB) and its mandates, teachers cannot simply close their doors and teach what they want to anymore. Imagine that you are a history teacher. You are not the biggest fan of geography and would much rather devote some additional time to culture—very valuable in today's global world. However, the state in which you work employs a lot of geography questions and not many culture questions on the state test. Would you better serve your students by continuing to focus on what you feel comfortable with as a teacher, or should you spend more time teaching a skill not your forte? Obviously you would need to spend more time on the geography skills and improve your own comfort level. You could call this teaching to the test, but we prefer to call it "best preparing students for the assessment" that in many cases students need to pass to graduate. Sometimes we truly need to put aside our own egos in order to become the best at what we do.

In your PLC you can discuss the instructional implications of such information. Does there need to be a refocusing of the curriculum map? Are all teachers qualified to teach the subjects required of them and, if not, what does the group need to do to make sure they do become qualified? There might even be a reshuffling of classrooms based on the information gained in these sessions. Remember as you work in your PLC that what should be at the forefront of all decisions is what is best for kids.

Getting a better understanding of the state assessment in your PLC makes it very clear what is (and maybe is not) expected to be taught by each individual teacher. This understanding allows each teacher to create a classroom environment which best prepares students to succeed on the high-stakes assessment, which is the ultimate goal of the SCORE Process.

If You Learn One Thing From This Chapter . . .

Know where your PLC is in regard to the understanding of the state standards and assessments because this is critical to the process of creating short-cycle formative assessments. You can use consensograms to figure out where the PLC is in this process, and then analyze both accordingly.

Part of this process involves creating a Taxonomy Table to figure out at what level of Bloom's Taxonomy the standard falls, as well as analyzing past state assessments to see which standards are assessed more than others. Both of these activities, when done well, will make later steps in the process that much easier. This, of course, will lead to greater functionality of the professional learning community.

4

Aligning the Curriculum

Organizing is what you do before you do something, so that when you do it, it's not all mixed up.

—A. A. Maline

As you go through the SCORE Process, for time management purposes, each step should be a separate PLC meeting. In other words, don't try to cover Steps 1 and 2 in a single, 1-hour meeting. It does not allow for much discussion or sharing and will result in a sloppy product. Trying to do too much in one sitting may risk overwhelming the members of the PLC and possibly cause burn out. This process will tax your brain, which is why it is professional development. With that in mind, the following is a reasonable timeline for a PLC working on short-cycle assessments, specifically using the SCORE Process:

Meeting 1—*Introductions/Identifying various group styles*
Meetings 2 & 3—Step 1: *Understanding the State Standards*
Meeting 4—Step 2: *Understanding the State Assessment*

You'll notice in this particular schedule two meetings were devoted to state standards because for this group a consensogram determined the PLC rated a 3 in regard to their comfort level of the state standards and they wanted to spend a little more time analyzing and identifying the different levels of Bloom's Taxonomy.

The next meeting should be devoted to Step 3 in the SCORE Process; the development of a pacing chart. (See Figure 4.1.) This is one of the more challenging meetings in the SCORE Process because now everyone must come to a consensus as to how these standards will be spread out over the school year. It reminds one of a Calvin and Hobbes cartoon where the main character, a plucky elementary kid named Calvin, has gotten into an argument with his dad. Both are yelling at one another and part ways with scowls on their faces. Calvin quips, "A good compromise leaves everyone mad." That's the way many people leave this meeting feeling. In this case though, compromise is necessary.

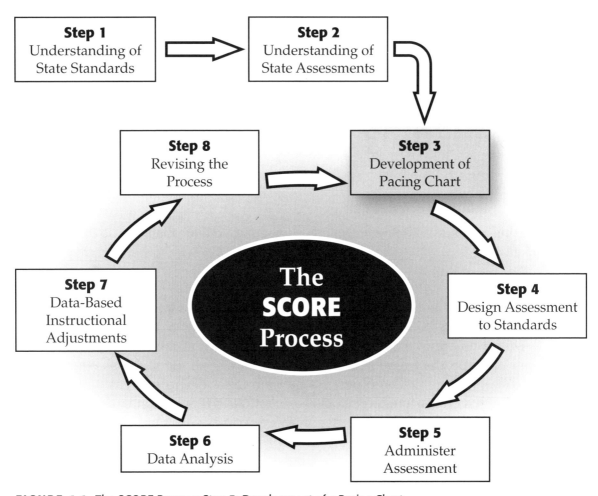

FIGURE 4.1 The SCORE Process: Step 3: Development of a Pacing Chart

Figuring Out Your Pacing Chart

Step 3 of the SCORE Process involves figuring out when you are going to teach and assess a particular standard during the course of the school year. As a PLC group, this involves sitting down and determining in which of the grading periods particular skills will be taught. Ideally speaking, if there are 40 standards that need to be taught, and there are four grading periods, then placing 10 standards per grading period would make sense. But that is in an ideal world. Reality is much different, and there are many factors to consider:

♦ Some standards take longer to teach than others.
♦ Some grading periods have the potential for more interruptions than others (e.g., winter time and snow days).
♦ Depending on when your state administers its test will influence when certain standards are taught. (i.e., if the test is given in March, waiting until the last

grading period to teach standards that will be found on that test would not be wise).
- Some standards will need to be taught in multiple grading periods.
- Students seem to be more attentive at different times in the year (try teaching a concept the week before spring break).
- There are certain standards students have difficulty with and these may have to be retaught in later grading periods.
- There are some standards that are easily forgotten and should be taught nearer to the test date to keep them fresh.

All of these factors need to be discussed and determined before placing standards on the pacing chart. A pacing chart is very similar to a curriculum map except it is more of a placement of when instruction and assessment will occur, whereas a curriculum map is more of a detailed plan of instructional strategies. That means if 12 standards are placed in the first section of the pacing chart, then those 12 standards need to be assessed on the first formative short-cycle assessment.

This fact needs to stay in the forefront as the discussion begins. Some teachers argue that certain skills, such as vocabulary and multiplication, need to be taught every grading period. But that is not what is being determined on a pacing chart. Certain skills can be taught all year long, but only need to be assessed maybe once or twice, depending on when information toward mastery is needed. In the PLC meeting, when a pacing chart is first developed, determining when the standard will be assessed on a formative assessment will, in turn, determine the placement of the standard on a pacing chart.

This can be difficult because people will have different ideas about when things need to be taught. Some will argue you should teach the standards in the order they appear in the textbook, while others feel very strongly about beginning with lower level thinking standards before moving into the higher level ones. Rarely does everyone agree. That is why compromise is so important within the PLC.

Regardless of which standard is placed where, it is important for all voices to be heard and for all rationales to be argued. Although many can live with not getting their way, it is difficult to deal with not getting their say. It is important in these meetings to maintain a balance between the north who tends to dominate the conversation, with the south who remains quiet so as not to rock the boat. One method for equal sharing may involve reading the standard aloud, and then having each person speak before another can chime in, suggesting where that standard should be placed. If there are some standards that the PLC members feel very strongly about, you might consider placing those first and filling in with the others. Another consideration might be to break the larger PLC into four smaller groups, with each one working on a different grading period, placing the standards as they deem appropriate. Then discussion with the whole group will be necessary to determine if there is overlap of the standards.

However the PLC decides to complete the pacing chart, keep in mind this is a process with a lot of give and take. Everyone needs to understand that the pacing chart should be flexible, not written in stone, where changes can be made fairly easily if the group sees things are not progressing according to plan.

Types of Pacing Charts

There is no incorrect way to set up your pacing chart as long as it makes sense to the PLC. We typically find schools divide it into grading periods so if your school is on 9-week sessions, you will have 4 divisions, and if you have 6-week sessions, you will have 6 divisions. The pacing chart could even be separated by semesters with only 2 divisions although this is a long time to go between short-cycle assessments. Figure 4.2 is an example of the most common pacing chart, a 4-section one. You will notice a number system used to identify the standards. We always suggest using these to make the pacing chart easier to read. It is a fairly simple system. The first number refers to the strand or overall topics in the subject area. For instance, in Pennsylvania, the English standards have been divided into the following categories or strands:

1. Learning to Read Independently
2. Reading Critically in All Content Areas
3. Reading, Analyzing, and Interpreting Literature
4. Types of Writing
5. Quality of Writing
6. Speaking and Listening
7. Characteristics and Function of the English Language
8. Research

Grade Level: 8   Subject Area: English

Grading Period 1 Standards	*Grading Period 2 Standards*	*Grading Period 3 Standards*	*Grading Period 4 Standards*
1-1	1-2	1-5	1-4
2 1	1-3	2-3	2-4 (discuss)
2-4 (infer)	2-2	2-7 (technology)	3-2
2-6	2-5	3-2	4-4
2-7 (dictionaries)	4-6	3-5	4-9
3-1	5-2	4-1	5-4
3-3	5-3	4-2	5-8
3-4	5-5	4-3	5-9
5-1	5-6	4-5	
	5-7	4-7	
		4-8	

FIGURE 4.2 Four-Section Pacing Chart

Under these strands are the standards that describe them such as these Grade 5 Reading, Analyzing, and Interpreting Literature standards:

3. Reading, Analyzing, and Interpreting Literature
   1. Read and understand works of literature.
   2. Compare the use of literary elements within and among texts, including characters, setting, plot, theme, and point of view.
   3. Describe how the author uses literary devices to convey meaning.
      - Sound techniques (e.g., rhyme, rhythm, meter, alliteration)
      - Figurative language (e.g., personification, simile, metaphor, hyperbole).
   4. Identify and respond to the effects of sound and structure in poetry (e.g., alliteration, rhyme, verse form).
   5. Analyze drama as information source, entertainment, persuasion, or transmitter of culture.
   6. Read and respond to nonfiction and fiction including poetry and drama.

Thus if 3-4 is put on the pacing chart, it refers to the following standard:

3. Reading, Analyzing, and Interpreting Literature
   4. Identify and respond to the effects of sound and structure in poetry (e.g., alliteration, rhyme, verse form).

Numbers, letters, or whatever else makes sense given your state's standards can be used, but it is most important that the coding be clear to the PLC members. We have worked with some groups that prefer to write the standards completely out. It is important to find a system that works best for everyone involved.

There are some things to consider when placing standards on your pacing chart:

♦ At what point do you want the information as to the student's progress in learning that particular standard?
♦ At what point would you expect the student to have "mastered" that standard?
♦ At what point would you begin to become concerned if that student had not "mastered" the standard?
♦ At what point would you feel it necessary to provide intervention for that standard?

Use these questions as a guide within your professional learning community as you create your pacing chart. We have provided a blank *Pacing Chart* on page 108 of the Blueprints section.

Identifying Power Standards

The general idea behind a pacing chart is to take all the standards for a given subject area and divide them up over the school year. However, some teachers do not feel the need to assess every single standard. They would rather focus on those standards that are the most important. These are called *power standards*. The trick is to correctly identify power standards. Just because a PLC becomes convinced a standard does not qualify as a power standard does not mean the state isn't going to have it on its high-stakes test. We suggest a three-pronged criteria to identify power standards.

Criteria #1—Skills needed for success in the content area
Criteria #2—Essential knowledge and skills that transfer across the curriculum
Criteria #3—Standards assessed on the state test

Once you identify power standards, you should not ignore the other standards. The idea is that you prioritize, not eliminate. All of the standards will still need to be taught and assessed in day-to-day practices, but the focus is on these power standards for the purposes of developing your formative short-cycle assessments.

Skills Needed for Success in the Content Area

The first criteria to consider when choosing power standards is determining what essential knowledge and skills are critical for a student to succeed in a specific content area. You can sit down as a group and have a general discussion concerning what skills the PLC feels are valuable based on teaching and educational experience. This type of work can best be done within a PLC that is content-based, but even if the PLC contains members of many different content areas and grade levels, this task can be fairly easy. The basic knowledge about the skills in this case would come from the teacher teaching in that content area. Then, all the members of the PLC could weigh in, asking clarifying questions and narrowing the focus on the skills.

An activity to determine the skills necessary for success in a content area is the Hope List activity. The activity begins with subject area teachers working together to answer the following question:

What are 5 skills you hope every student graduating from this school has with regard to your subject area?

Allow group members some time to discuss and debate this question while compiling the list. Make sure to qualify that these are content skills, not behavioral or work study skills such as being polite, completing homework, or being able to function in society (although those things would be nice). To develop power standards, it is imperative in this first step of the process to concentrate on content-specific skills only. Even though elementary teachers may be taking part in this, they might feel there are building blocks they impart to students early on that should be carried through to graduation, such as reading skills and math basics. If you have a particularly large PLC, you might want to break these groups up even further rather than have a group of ten or more. Try to mix together various grade levels such as elementary with high school teachers rather than letting them sit with their grade levels. This of course presents its own set of challenges: if forming a PLC across different schools, you will really need to think outside the box as far as scheduling meetings, since the two groups are often on very different schedules. Having a half or full day of professional development sessions worked into the school calendar is a good way to do this.

When the group members have compiled their Hope Lists, have them organize them on chart paper to share with the rest of the group. If working with a multiple subject-area PLC, you may end up with several different lists. An example of a Social Studies Hope List is shown below:

- ◆ Students will have a global awareness.
- ◆ Students will be able to read a map.
- ◆ Students will understand that history repeats itself.
- ◆ Students will understand the importance of the Constitution.
- ◆ Students will know the history of our city.

Notice in this list there are a mixture of basic skills and concept skills. It's perfectly fine to have both of these included. Remind participants to think of this as everything they hope for. There is a blank *Hope List* in the Blueprints section on page 109.

Across the Curriculum

Now that the important skills for each subject area have been identified, the next step in the power standards process is for the PLC to figure out what essential knowledge and skills are valuable in multiple content areas. In other words, what skills, when mastered by students, will enable them to be successful in all content areas? The ability of reading comprehension is important in every class, not just in language arts, for example. Think of the directions you read for math, which must be understood in order to do the problems or the comprehension required to understand an experiment in science. All of these require the ability to comprehend, thus the skill of reading comprehension is a skill that would carry across the curriculum.

For this part of the PLC process, teachers need not be in their subject area groups and, in fact, it might be advantageous to divide the PLC into smaller groups with a mix of the subject areas to get different perspectives. Instruct the smaller groups to brainstorm cross-curricular skills together. Once again, remind them that this is a skill-based activity. Avoid answers like bringing a pencil to class, coming to school on time, or being motivated. Here are some types of skills this list might include:

- Students will be able to infer.
- Students will be able to understand what they read.
- Students will be able to read maps, charts, and graphs.
- Students will be organized in their writing.
- Students will be able to use a dictionary.
- Students will have legible handwriting.
- Students will be able to back up an opinion with evidence.
- Students will be able to compare and contrast.

These are just some essential skills teachers could come up with. An easy tool for sorting after brainstorming is to place the skills on sticky notes and cluster them in groups according to likeness. This will indicate which ones appear most often. The group should make a list of the skills they feel are the most important. Time should be given for sharing and debating the ideas. This may not happen quickly. What you are doing is one of those things teachers never get the opportunity to do: converse and collaborate. It's important to let it happen in a timely manner.

The State Test

Now that your PLC has figured out what the most important subject-specific and cross-curricular skills are, it is time to see what the state feels is important. It makes sense these would be one and the same but occasionally there are some differences. The good news is if you followed the steps from chapter 3, this activity is already complete. The tally marks indicating frequency of standards on the state test can be used to show how many times certain standards are used. Use the tally information to continue the process for determining power standards:

1. Within your subject area/grade level group, go over your analysis of the state assessment from the past few years.
2. Which standards or skills repeat themselves the most?
3. Which standards or skills do not appear to be present?
4. *Essential Question:* What are the essential skills a student would need by the end of the school year in order to be successful on the state assessment?

If this activity was not completed back in chapter 3, it will need to be at this time in order to effectively identify the power standards. This is an important step to take because the state has the ultimate authority as the creator of the high-stakes test, which most often is the indicator of academic success of the student.

Prioritizing the Power Standards

With the three criteria having been covered, the final step in developing the power standards is to integrate the information collected and decide on the most important standards for your subject area/grade level. Remember, identifying power standards is not about "eliminating" standards, but "prioritizing" them. In many cases, the PLC will find those standards the state focuses on are the same ones the teachers deemed to be important. Occasionally there will be some standards the state considers important that the group hasn't considered, or vice versa, and these should be included on the pacing chart. Your power standards pacing chart might look something like Figure 4.3. Notice this list has fewer standards than the original pacing chart, not to mention some standards were split in two such as 5-8, which covers both irony and point of view, and 3-3 which is adjusting speed and clauses/phrases. Also, there are some standards such as 2-3, infer meaning, and 3-1, reading comprehension, which are definitely standards that fall in the "across the curriculum" category, so they are important enough to assess more than once. After the list has been compiled within your PLC, it is important to spend a little more time discussing it, especially if there are there any additional standards that need to be identified as power standards.

Once the power standards have been identified, everyone in the school who comes into contact with students concerning that subject area should be given a copy. This means not just the teachers who are members of the PLC, but special education teachers, ESL teachers, tutors, gifted pull-out, and any other person in the system who helps to teach the subject area. It is important not to let anyone slip through the cracks. We have provided a tool for you to use to share the information. It is called the *What-How-Who-When Chart* and you can find it on page 110 in the Blueprints for the Process section. This will help to ensure that the proper people are aware of the work of the PLC.

Grade Level: 8   Subject Area: English

Grading Period 1 Standards	*Grading Period 2 Standards*	*Grading Period 3 Standards*	*Grading Period 4 Standards*
2-3 (infer meaning) 3-1 (reading comprehension) 3-3 (adjusting speed) 5-2 (setting) 5-3 (conflict) 5-6 (genre) 5-8 (irony)	2-2 (responses to lit.) 3-3 (clauses/phrases) 4-1 (organizational patterns) 4-7 (public documents) 5-7 (irony) 5-8 (point of view)	2-3 (infer meaning) 2-5 (Greek/Latin roots) 3-4 (parallel structure) 4-1 (rhetorical devices) 4-4 (propaganda/bias) 5-6 (subgenres, satire, parody, allegory) 5-7 (analyze characteristics)	2-3 (infer meaning) 2-5 (Greek/Latin roots) 3-1 (reading comprehension) 5-3 (parallel plots/subplots) 5-3 (pacing action) 5-4 (universal themes)

FIGURE 4.3 Power Standards Pacing Chart

If You Learn One Thing From This Chapter . . .

Figure out as a group when you are going to assess what standard and plot this out on a pacing chart. This puts everyone on the same page in regard to when to teach and assess certain standards. Understand that if students are going to be assessed on these standards at the end of the grading period, it is the responsibility of the teacher to present them beforehand. Know that just because a standard is not mentioned, it can still be addressed in that grading period. There are standards that will need to be taught throughout the entire year. Placement on the pacing chart simply means that standard will be assessed at the end of that grading period with a formative short-cycle assessment.

As a PLC you might decide to identify power standards. These are the standards seen as the most important within a subject area. Development of the power standards does not mean the elimination of the other standards, rather it is a process of prioritization based on teacher expertise and a thorough analysis of the state assessment.

Once the work of the PLC with regard to the pacing chart and the power standards has been completed, it is important to notify the appropriate people and make sure everyone is on the same page for maximum student achievement.

5

Writing Assessments

One should not aim at being possible to understand, but at being impossible to misunderstand.

— Quintilian (Marcus Fabius Quintilianus, 1st century, AD)

Writing assessments is the point where most people want to start the formative assessment process; after all, the entire point is to create short-cycle assessments. But if your PLC has followed the first three steps of the SCORE Process, then they have laid the valuable groundwork needed to write quality assessments designed to help improve student learning. A house cannot be built until you lay down a strong foundation. That is what the understanding of the state standards and the analysis of the state assessment are: a quality foundation on which to build a strong set of assessments. Without this strong foundation, the house will fall apart in a short period of time. Likewise, you would not begin building a house without a good blueprint or plan. Otherwise you wouldn't know where to put what. That is why a Pacing Chart is needed, to provide the plan for building the assessment. Now that you have this foundation and blueprint, it is time to begin construction of your assessments.

Design Assessment to Standards

Armed with your Pacing Chart, your PLC can now begin to write assessments. (See Figure 5.1.) Ideally, the PLC will go down the Pacing Chart, writing questions that address each standard. Once all of the standards have been covered with a question, you should have a formative short-cycle assessment. Of course, we all know nothing is as simple as it should be. You have to consider multiple questions for a single standard to ensure a particularly important skill is understood by the student, or you might have a standard that has several skills within it that cannot be addressed by a single question. An example of this is seen in the following from the Missouri Math Standards:

Compare the properties of *linear, exponential,* and *quadratic* functions (include domain and range).

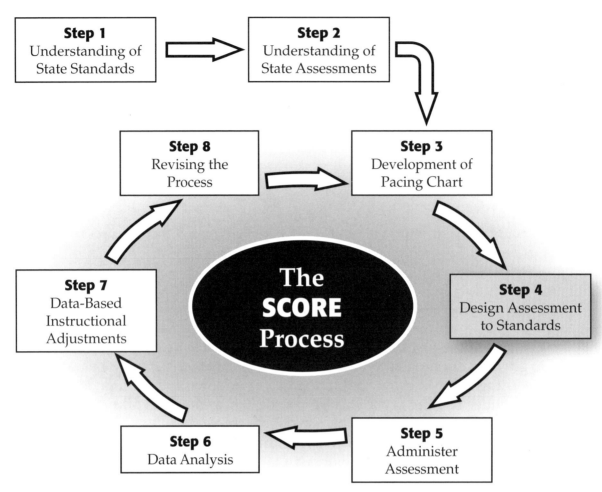

FIGURE 5.1 SCORE Process-Step 4: Design Assessment to Standards

There is a lot going on in this standard and it may take three or four questions to make sure students have mastered all of the concepts and skills. A teacher wouldn't ask a single question covering linear function and assume because the student got that one skill, the student understands exponential and quadratic functions as well. There would be a rude awakening if the state were to ask a question concerning exponential functions. It is imperative that each part of a standard is instructed and assessed.

We also recommend that no matter how many standards you have instructed in a given grading period, your assessment should be 15 to 30 questions long. An assessment of this length will give the teacher a good feel for whether students have mastered the material or not. Fewer than 15 questions might not give you enough information to create valid data. Many more than 30 questions and you risk pushing the boundary on the "short" aspect of short-cycle assessment.

Let's use an example from the last chapter. Figure 5.2 is the Pacing Chart for the first grading period: Being that there are nine standards, you know you will need to have at least nine questions on your short-cycle assessment. As a Reading PLC, you

Reading

Grading Period 1 Standards
1-1 2-1 2-4 (infer) 2-6 2-7 (dictionaries) 3-1 3-3 3-4 5-1

FIGURE 5.2 Pacing Chart

would need to decide which standards might need additional questions. Making those determinations before writing the questions will indicate exactly how many questions the group will write.

How to Work as a Group on Short-Cycle Assessments

There are a couple of different approaches you can take to writing the assessment as a PLC. Each has its advantages and disadvantages; you just need to determine which one is a better fit.

The first approach is writing the assessment as a large group, which is a key advantage in that everyone contributes to the development of each question. When everyone's voice is heard, the expertise of the entire group is utilized, and everyone in the PLC will become familiar with each question on the assessment. Discussion may occur around how that particular standard is taught in the classroom, opening the opportunity for the sharing of ideas. The disadvantage is that this method takes time. If you have nine people in your grade level/subject area PLC and all these voices need to be heard, the process can bog down, especially if the group members do not work well together, or even with a group who likes to talk a lot. We would recommend using this method with a PLC that works well together and doesn't get mired in discussions that veer off topic.

Another approach is the divide-and-conquer method. If you have nine members in your PLC, put them in groups of three and have each group write five to seven questions, assigning each group different standards. More questions will be written in a shorter amount of time. Discussion can still be interactive, but in a smaller group it will be more focused. A disadvantage to writing an assessment like this is the questions are pieced together. One group might write their questions very differently than the other group, and slapping them together may make for a disjointed assessment. Also, not everyone will be familiar with all the questions. There might be a standard one teacher does not understand as well as she would like, and by not having to write a question concerning that standard, she will not improve this deficiency. This method works best for groups with a time limit. Although a faster way to write questions, it may not be the most effective way if collaboration is your main goal.

A combination of the two methods might be a good option, having various groups take different standards, then swapping and editing each other's questions. Using this method, everyone will be exposed to the questions and have the opportunity to take part in the discussion.

At this point, let us look at some ineffective ways to write a short-cycle assessment within a PLC. The route we see many teachers wanting to take is piecing together old state assessments or pulling questions from workbooks or study aid websites. This is certainly the easiest way to compile questions. As some people have argued, why reinvent the wheel if someone has already written a good question concerning the standard? If a student is assigned a certain set of math problems and he is able to get the answers from someone else, this serves the purpose for completing the work, correct? Of course, no teacher would accept this, saying the student won't learn in this manner. This is a process, and part of the professional development occurs by going through the process. Learning how to write the questions is just as valuable as producing a quality assessment. The more familiar teachers become in working with the standards, the more comfortable they become as experts, able to transfer this knowledge to the classroom, and, ultimately, to the students.

The Format of the Questions

Once the PLC decides how to write the assessment, everybody needs to be on the same page with regard to the format. The formative short-cycle assessments are designed to model the state assessment. The comparison here is if you are trying to prepare athletes for a football game, you don't practice on a baseball diamond. You put them on the football field and make the practice as real as the situation they will be encountering. Similarly, if your state assessment does not use the question formats of true-or-false, matching, or fill in the blank, neither should your short-cycle assessments. Students need to be given practice with the types of questions they will see on the high-stakes test.

The PLC should have already discovered what question format your state uses by the analysis of the past state assessments in Step 2 of the SCORE Process. Typically questions come in these forms:

◆ **Multiple Choice**: These are questions where students have four possible choices (some states such as Ohio have three choices for 3rd grade and below).

- **Response Grid**: These are typically used with math assessments and only in certain states. Here the students work a math problem and bubble in the correct answer. (See Figure 5.3.)
- **Multipart Constructed Response**: These are essentially essay questions, where students must write out a short response. Depending on the state, some have two-part, three-part, or four-part responses. It is important to figure out what combination your state uses and train students to look for them. That way they are answering all the parts required.
- **Writing Prompts**: These are longer essays for which students do not necessarily have to answer questions using knowledge, but show their writing ability through their responses. These are usually open-ended, opinion-based prompts and most often found on writing assessments.

Whatever the format, it is important to figure out what your state does and model this. Even the ratio of questions needs to be considered. If a majority of the questions on the

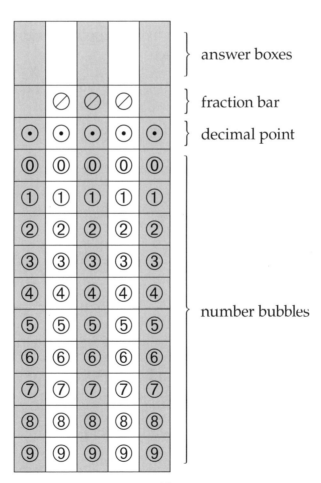

FIGURE 5.3 Response Grid

state assessment are multiple choice, your formative short-cycle assessment should be the same. There is a worksheet in the Blueprints section on page 111 called *Questions Conversion Chart* to determine this ratio.

How to Write the Questions

As you begin to write questions in your PLC, you will find some people are natural-born question writers, while others have little to no experience. You might possibly find some who think they are natural-born question writers, but are not used to writing questions in the format the state uses. We will assume everyone is new to the process and will provide basic strategies for writing questions. You may have determined your group is experienced enough not to need this section, but it might not hurt to review to make sure everyone is on the same page.

Armed with the Taxonomy Table to determine the level of the questions, and the Pacing Chart to determine which standards will be addressed, you can begin to write the questions. The easiest way to write a question is simply to take the statement that is the standard and turn it into a question. For example, consider this standard from the 8th Grade South Carolina Science curriculum:

Explain how the surface features of the Sun may affect Earth.

This could become a question with the addition of just a few simple words.

How can the surface features of the Sun affect the Earth?

You have the basis for a very good question that certainly covers the standard because it *is* the standard. Now you can take this question and turn it into a two-part constructed response:

What are two ways the surface features of the Sun can affect the Earth? Be sure to be detailed in your choices.

Or a multiple-choice question:

Which of the following is *not* a way the surface features of the Sun can affect the Earth?

    a. **affects the climate**
    b. **affects the rotation**
    c. **affects the tides**
    d. **affects the seasons**

Changing the standard itself into a question is a great place to start. You can try doing this within your PLC with a couple of the standards you will be working with using the *Standard to Question Activity* on page 112 in the Blueprints section just to make sure everyone understands.

That is the basic formula for writing a good question. Like most things, the more you do it, the better you will become. Writing questions at first might seem like a slow-going process but with practice comes experience which breeds quality. Of course, the added bonus when you write a question to a standard is that you better understand how to instruct that standard.

If you feel your group needs more guidance with question writing or for a more detailed explanation of how to write questions for each of the levels of Bloom's, you can check out our other books *Short Cycle Assessments: Improving Student Achievement through Formative Assessment* (2008) or *Critical Thinking and Formative Assessments: Increasing the Rigor in Your Classroom* (2009).

If you have completed the first few steps of the SCORE Process and have established a good group dynamic, the writing of the actual assessments should not be too time consuming. You should be able to pound out a rough draft in the matter of a few hours. Keep in mind that you could assign the questions to group members to develop outside of the PLC.

The Importance of Editing

It is important to note that the first time writing questions will lead to a rough draft, and the editing should take just as long and be just as involved as the initial writing. We highly recommend the writing and editing be two separate meetings with your PLC. It is difficult to edit properly when your brain has been turned to mush from writing questions all day. It is a good idea to put some physical space between these activities: even just a day is helpful, so that people are looking at the questions with fresh eyes.

There are formatting issues to consider when editing your formative short-cycle assessment:

♦ Do you have 15 to 30 questions?
♦ Is the spacing adequate?
♦ If you used a reading prompt is the text clear?
♦ Is the font size and format comparable to the state assessment?
♦ Are the graphics of high quality considering this is going to be run through a copy machine and made duller?
♦ Are there instances where half the question is at the bottom of a page but the other half is cut off and on top of the next page?
♦ Is there a good distribution of multiple choice, constructed response, etc., according to your Questions Conversion Chart?

◆ Have you provided an answer sheet for students that looks similar to the state assessment? (Resist the urge to use Scantron if the state doesn't.)
◆ Are the directions for administration clear?

Here are some content issues to consider:

◆ Do you use the verb of the standard?
◆ Is the question clear?
◆ Is the question at the proper level of Bloom's according to your Taxonomy Table?
◆ Does the question address the standard?
◆ Do two-point questions have two clear parts to them? Four-point questions four parts, and so on?
◆ Are all the standards from your Pacing Chart covered by this assessment?

We have included some revising and editing sheets in the Blueprints for the Process section. Here are descriptions of how to use each of these protocols within your PLC:

◆ *Assessment Analysis Worksheet*: As a group, go through the assessment, question by question, analyzing each one. You need to determine, as a group, which standard the question covers, the format of the question, and the level of Bloom's at which the question is asked. This is an especially effective tool for those big picture east people because it looks at the assessment as a whole. This will take some time but it will lead to a thorough analysis and point out any major holes in the assessment. (Blueprints page 113)
◆ *Assessment Checklist*: This is for the group to use once the assessment is in its final draft and last-minute revisions are being considered. We have seen some groups project the assessment up on a whiteboard using an LCD projector and examine the test question by question as a PLC with this checklist in front of them. Having so many eyes to edit will catch mistakes one person might not see. (Blueprints page 114)
◆ *Pacing Chart Confirmation*: This tool is a final checklist to make sure the standards from the Pacing Chart have all been addressed on the assessment. It is also an opportunity to indicate as a group what standards were not addressed in the assessment and how those standards will be otherwise assessed in the classroom. An example of this can be seen using the following standard:

Take various roles within the group.

This would be difficult to assess with a question on a short-cycle assessment, but could be observed in day-to-day activities using a checklist or rubric. This will also allow the PLC an opportunity to discuss different strategies for assessing student skills of these performance standards. (Blueprints page 115)

◆ *Writing/Reading/General Assessment Checklists*: These are three general checklists to make sure the assessment models the state assessment. Using these checklists, PLCs will know to include such things as poetry and nonfiction selections for reading and prewriting activities for writing, as well as graphic organizers and grade-level reading passages for other subject area assessments. Your PLC can use whichever checklist fits the appropriate subject area for the assessment they are developing (Blueprints pages 116, 117, and 118).

Whatever method you use to edit, it is important to have a short-cycle assessment that looks as professional and models as much as possible the high-stakes test your state administers.

It is also important that the questions be clear. Like the quote at the beginning of this chapter, you don't want there to be any misunderstandings about what the question is asking. You want to be sure students are clear on this and you are evaluating their skills, not tricking them with confusing questions.

These steps for writing assessments should be followed for the second, third, and fourth assessments as well (or however many short-cycle assessments the PLC has decided to create). It is important to know that writing the first assessment is probably going to be the most difficult because you are getting used to the process and figuring out the question-writing ability of each member. Once that first assessment is under your belt, the remaining ones should go much smoother within your PLC.

If You Learn One Thing From This Chapter . . .

With the Taxonomy Table, state assessment analysis, and strong group dynamics, writing the short-cycle assessment should be a matter of figuring out the best way to write the 15 to 30 questions as a group. One of the largest obstacles when working on a project like this is getting everyone on the same page and these three items should have most group members within the PLC rowing the boat together.

Editing is nearly as important as writing the short-cycle assessment. Make sure you go through your formative short-cycle assessment with a fine-tooth comb, keeping in mind that questions should be clear and the assessment itself should mirror the state's as much as possible. You want students to be as familiar as possible with the format, style, and language of this high-stakes test. As your PLC becomes more adept at question writing, the entire process will become much smoother, and both teacher confidence in question writing and the ability to instruct more effectively will occur.

6

Administering and Grading
the Assessments

Context is always as relevant as concept.

—Terry Olson

Now that the assessments have been written by the PLC, it may feel as if the process is finished. Unfortunately the work is only half done. There is still plenty left to do to prepare students for high-stakes testing. In the introduction of this book we promised formative short-cycle assessments would have four benefits, the four E's. They looked like this:

1. **Exposure:** To give students planned and purposeful exposure to the standards and formats.
2. **Expertise:** To develop expertise in each teacher's ability to ask higher-level questions, base instructional decisions for delivery on performance data, and collaborate for curricular direction across grade levels.
3. **Endurance:** To build resilience and endurance for each student to be able to a) sit through the test and b) work through difficult questions.
4. **Empower:** To empower students and their parents to become responsible decision makers for learning.

Up until this point, the *exposure* has been accomplished through the use of the Pacing Chart, which makes learning the standards intentional for students. The *expertise* of the teachers has been increased through the work within the PLC—the creation of the Taxonomy Table, the writing of the actual assessments, and the sharing of ideas and collaboration. Now comes the time to work on the *endurance* of the students. This can be done by administering the assessments in a purposeful manner.

When your PLC rolls out the first assessment, it needs to be an organized effort that models the state testing process as much as possible. This is also part of the exposure to the test. If students are comfortable with testing conditions and become familiar with them, it will not seem so foreign when the state tests are given. This will be a substantial advantage for the students.

Administering the Assessment

This brings us to Step 5 of the SCORE Process, administering the assessment, Figure 6.1. During this step, the PLC will want to develop a plan to administer the assessment. This plan should be well thought out with several important considerations. Some of these are:

- ◆ How does the state administer its tests?
  - • Two in a day, one a day, all in a single week, spread out over 2 weeks?
- ◆ Is everyone on board and knows the plan?
- ◆ Are there consistent directions for the assessments?
- ◆ Does the regular school schedule need to be altered?
  - • Have the proper people (administrators, specials teachers, lunch room staff, speech) been notified?
- ◆ Are the rooms being used similar to the setup students will experience with the state tests?

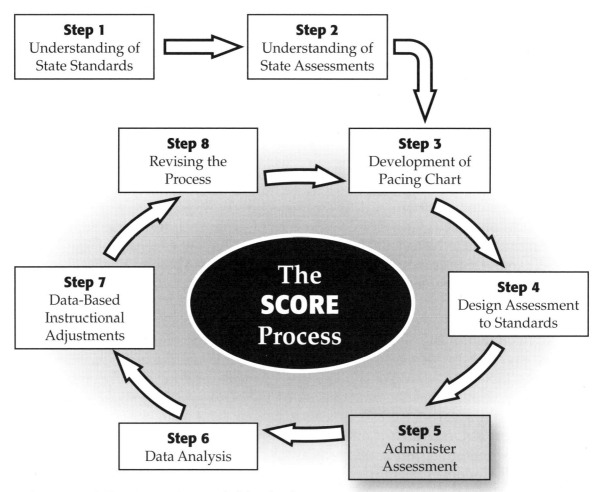

FIGURE 6.1 SCORE Process-Step 5:Administering the Assessment

- ◆ Have you considered accommodations for those students who need them?
  - • Are there students who need the test read to them or need someone to write for them?
- ◆ Are there grade levels or teachers not taking part in this? If so, are they aware of the process and will they make sure the noise level in their classrooms and hallways will not be distracting?

The PLC should hold a meeting to discuss these considerations rather than having someone decree them such as an administrator or curriculum coordinator. Through discussions over these decisions and the pounding out of a schedule, teachers will be able to establish the proper assessment-administration environment.

Creating the Proper Environment

There are several things to consider when creating the proper environment for the administration of the assessment. You might view the formative short-cycle assessment as a dress rehearsal for the high-stakes state test. In a proper dress rehearsal, everything is done in the exact same manner as the final performance. You have the costumes, you move the scenery, you speak the lines loudly. The cast is put through everything they will experience on opening night; the only difference is there is no audience to judge them. Similarly, the only thing that should be different in the formative short-cycle assessments experience is the lack of judgment. The purpose of a dress rehearsal for a play is to notice any problems and fix them before the audience sees them. In the same vein, short-cycle assessments should be used to locate gaps in student skills so they can be addressed before the state test.

When creating the proper environment, everything from the morning announcements, to the restroom schedule, to the classroom set up, should be the same. For instance, if during the high-stakes test, students are seated no more than 20 to a room and must sign out in order to use the restroom, the formative short-cycle assessment environment should be the same. If the state assessment has a time limit, which most of them do, then a comparable time limit should be established for the short-cycle assessment. Since this is a short-cycle assessment, without as many questions as the actual high-stakes test, an appropriate time limit needs to be determined. For instance, if your state allots 60 minutes to take the Social Studies test, and if you have half as many questions on your short-cycle assessment, then a time limit of 30 minutes may be appropriate. This serves to get students used to managing their time.

Because you are unfolding these formative short-cycle assessments in a PLC, it is important as a group that you are consistent. All teachers giving the common assessment will want to do so on the same day. You don't want some teachers giving it on one day, and others on another day. For example, everyone who is giving the 7th grade science assessment should be giving it on the same day and around the same time.

	Monday	*Tuesday*	*Wednesday*	*Thursday*	*Friday*
Week 1	5th Reading	6th Reading	5th Math	6th Math	
Week 2	5th Science		5th Social Studies		

FIGURE 6.2 Schedule

When the schedule is drawn up, it should model the state schedule as well. If the state math assessment is normally given in the morning as a school, all the math teachers should do the same with their short-cycle assessments. A schedule might look like Figure 6.2. Notice that whoever set up the schedule avoided Friday, thinking students might be burnt out by the end of the week. Your PLC will want to consider these things when setting the assessment schedule. The PLC should stagger the schedule much like this example. This will build student endurance in small quantities so that once students go through three cycles of this process, they will be good and ready for the state assessment at year's end.

Something as simple as making sure the hallways are quiet and there are no interruptions in the classroom or announcements blaring to disrupt student focus are important. Posting a sign outside your door so people do not enter is a small thing that goes a long way. The *Testing Do Not Disturb* sign in the Blueprints section on page 119 can be copied and posted on doors.

Teacher attitude also goes a long way in setting the environment with students. If a teacher acts as though the assessment is inconsequential, the students will pick up on this fairly quickly and emulate this attitude. Consequently, the data received will not reflect the true ability of the students. Teachers need to stress the importance of these assessments. One way to do this is to tell students data from the short-cycle assessments will determine the course of the year—in other words, whether something will be retaught or not. Making sure all teachers administering the assessment are on board is very important to creating this environment.

What materials students are allowed to use also needs to be consistent. If the state assessment allows students to use a calculator on the high-stakes test, students should be allowed to do the same on the short-cycle assessments. On the converse side, if calculators are not permitted, the same goes for the short-cycle assessments. It is important to find out what the state does and does not allow at each grade level and model those conditions.

The directions being consistent and clear are also crucial to the positive testing environment. Every teacher should read the same set of directions, and run the classroom the same way. Although this will take a certain amount of coordination, it will be extremely beneficial to the students to develop a routine with assessments, thus helping students to develop exposure to the test. The *Directions for Short-Cyle Assessment* in the Blueprints section on page 120 will help with this.

Creating the Answer Key

Although this is something that could have been addressed when creating the actual assessment, we chose to discuss it here because this is where its importance is really felt. The answer key to the formative short-cycle assessment must be clear in that numerous teachers in the PLC will be using it and have to understand it. This should not be a problem with multiple choice or response grid questions where there are definite answers. This gets a bit more hazy when constructed responses are involved.

Many times when a teacher creates an answer key, the answer is more of a sketchy outline that reminds the teacher of what she is looking for. Yet with several people using the answer key, it has to be detailed and clear, even going so far as to provide examples to determine what is and is not acceptable for constructed response questions.

The answer key, just like the assessment itself, should be written by the group and discussed to make sure everyone is on the same page. Take the following question considering inference for 9th Grade English:

What might the two roads represent or symbolize? Which road would you have taken and why?

There are a lot of possible answers and all of them cannot be included in the answer key. What can be done however is to give the person grading an idea of what the question is looking for. The answer key might look like this:

Answer:
1 point—Accept all reasonable responses that have a contrast to one another. Examples might include:

- **Follow the crowd/Do your own thing**
- **Go with the flow/going against the grain**
- **Doing the right thing/doing the wrong thing**
- **Taking the easy way/challenging yourself**

1 point—Once students have presented each road, they must select one of them. Student must explain why they took that road and the result of this choice.

You do not want to leave too much to interpretation when it comes to an answer key. When there is a question that requires a student opinion, often time teachers will put in the answer key:

Answers will vary.

A better answer would be:

Student will include an opinion and back this up with details and/or examples pertaining to the question. Student answer should not contain any opinion but their own.

It is also a good idea to be clear in a multipart question about exactly what criteria it takes to earn each point, for instance, for the following question:

Mr. Jones is designing a house to be built in Arizona. Conservation of natural resources is very important to him. What would be the best energy source Mr. Jones could use for his home that would be environmentally friendly? What might be an advantage and a disadvantage of using the energy source you have chosen? What might be another energy source that could be used?

Your answer key should look something like this:

Answer:
1 pt.—(for one source) solar; wind; biomass; geothermal; hydroelectric

1pt.—(advantages) solar—plentiful, renewable, less pollution; wind—renewable; biomass—renewable, accessible, less pollution; geothermal—renewable, less pollution; hydroelectric—renewable, less pollution

1 pt.—(disadvantages) solar—costly; wind—dependability, not attractive; biomass—takes away land; geothermal—costly; hydroelectric—not readily accessible, destructible of habitat

1 pt.—for naming one other alternative

Sometimes a way to describe appropriate answers is to describe an answer that would be unacceptable. In the question,

What was your favorite part of the book and why?

you would want to include in the answer key,

Unacceptable Answer: "Because I liked it" or "The cover."

Sometimes the unacceptable example tells the grader more than a dozen examples of acceptable answers.

The PLC should go over the answer key together to ensure it makes sense to all. Someone in the group could read the question while another person answers with the answer key aloud, and the group can discuss and decide if it indeed clearly answers the question.

Whatever method you choose, always keep the following in mind: If someone not involved in the PLC and the development of the assessment had to grade the formative short-cycle assessment, would they be able to do so with consistency using the answer key provided?

Anchoring

When the students have finally taken the assessment, it is important the grading be consistent to make the data valid. What you don't want is one teacher who is a tough grader, giving a student a 2 out of 4 on a constructed response, while another one who is more lenient awards a similar response a 3 out of 4. The results of the assessment could be skewed. One point may not seem like much but if there are 6 to 7 constructed responses, that is a 6 to 7 point differential. In addition, in many states 3 out of 4 is considered mastery while a 2 out of 4 is not, so the student who had the lenient grader may actually need to be retaught the skill—something the data would not support.

The way to prevent this is anchoring. Anchoring is when several people grade the same assessment and compare how many points each awarded. If there is some disagreement, this is discussed until everyone is on the same page as to how to grade that constructed response. It is important to have a few rounds of anchoring and discussion to set the standard for what type of response will be awarded what level of points. *Anchoring Examples for Constructed Responses* in the Blueprints section, p. 122 show examples from the Maryland School Assessment.

Another way to conduct an anchoring session is to project example student responses on overheads and have teachers discuss how they would grade them with copies of the answer key in front of them. The group should establish student examples for all point levels. For instance, if the question is a 4-point question, you will want to establish a 0-, 1-, 2-, 3-, and 4-point examples. Doing a couple of these would be helpful to guide graders.

One thing we highly recommend is grading in a PLC meeting since all of the other work on the short-cycle assessments has been done as a group. This way you can spend the beginning of the meeting anchoring, then the remaining portion grading as a group and discussing issues that might arise. We would recommend not grading the students in your own class, but switching with another teacher as an impartial grader. Grading in this way will ensure that the inherent bias, whether good or bad, we associate with the knowledge we have of our students won't factor into the assessing.

If You Learn One Thing From This Chapter . . .

Consistency is the name of the game in this part of the SCORE Process. The administration of the formative short-cycle assessment needs to be consistent, with every teacher following similar procedures and having a consistent positive attitude toward the test. The schedule also needs to be consistent with what the state will do with the high-stakes testing schedule.

You will need this consistency throughout the creation of the answer key, making sure it is perfectly clear what a proper answer is, and in some cases, is not. Once your PLC has its answer key, use it to consistently grade the assessments, making sure to be on the same page as to what constitutes the various point levels. A good session of anchoring assessments will go a long way in establishing this.

7

Data Analysis

A statistical analysis, properly conducted, is a delicate dissection of uncertainties, a surgery of suppositions.

—M. J. Moroney

After the administering and grading of the assessments, it is sort of like Christmas Day after all the presents have been opened. There is that immediate letdown from all the build up of the previous months leading up to the event. What do we do now? The simple answer is, now you play with the presents you opened, namely the data generated from the assessments. It is important not to let down because this is the most important part of the process. This is where you as the teacher will learn more about your students and their skills. It will determine how your classroom will look over the course of the rest of the year, and if done properly within your PLC, it will improve your own ability as a teacher, which will lead to increased student achievement.

Looking at the Results

Data is one of those words in education that gets a bad name. Many times we as teachers don't know what to do with it. So what if a student's SAI is a 103 or her score on last year's high-stakes test was proficient, or that she has a high raw ability score on the ITBS? You as the teacher have to meet this student where she is now, figuring out how best to teach her. How are numbers going to help with that?

This is why one of the most important parts of the SCORE Process is the analysis of the information. (See Figure 7.1.) This data is valuable because a) it is immediate, and b) it is useful to your specific classroom instruction. Since the formative short-cycle assessments are based on standards your PLC decided to instruct in a particular grading period, teachers can see just how well the students performed on these standards. Also because these are formative short-cycle assessments, the results are going to help determine how teachers will teach the next grading period. Of course the teachers will be instructing the standards that the PLC has determined it will be teaching, but there will also be instances based on the data when a teacher will have to reteach a concept,

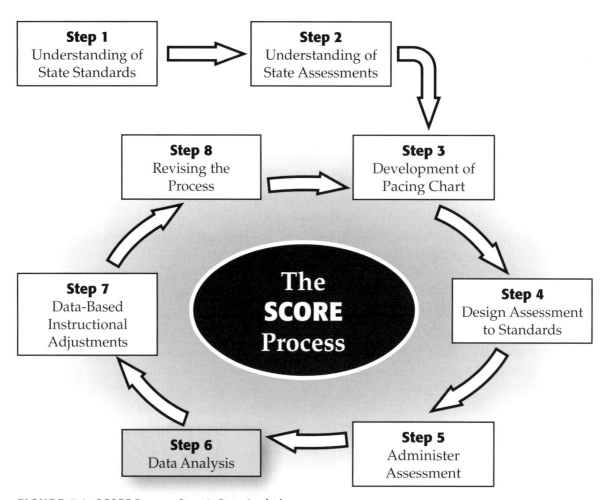

FIGURE 7.1 SCORE Process-Step 6: Data Analysis

or when the teacher will want to group students together because the data has shown a pattern of having difficulty with a particular strand.

Organizing the Data

Before you can begin to look at the data as a PLC, it has to be organized in some manner. This can be done in several different ways. One way is for a single person, a curriculum coordinator or person who is heading the PLC, to take all of the data accumulated in the grading session and organize it as one large group. Another way to organize the data is to have each individual teacher do so for his or her own classroom. Rather than one person organizing results for 150 students, this method would have five teachers organizing the data for 30 students apiece. Yet another way is to see if a couple of teachers in the group who have shown an aptitude for organizing data or enjoy crunching numbers might sort out the information the assessment provides for the PLC.

However you decide to organize the data, you also need to consider how to display it. The following are several different graphs that will easily and effectively display the data for the best possible analysis:

Student Profile Graph

The student profile graph (Figure 7.2) profiles every student who took the assessment and illustrates how each one scored overall. By gathering this information, the PLC can determine whether a majority of students are "getting it" and if not, which ones specifically are not. This graph lists every student on the X axis and his or her total percentage score on the Y axis. A bar graph charts how the individual student performed on the short-cycle assessment. How to set this up can be found on the Blueprints page *Directions for Student Profile Graph* along with a blank on pages 128–130. This graph is effective because it allows teachers to pinpoint which individual students need

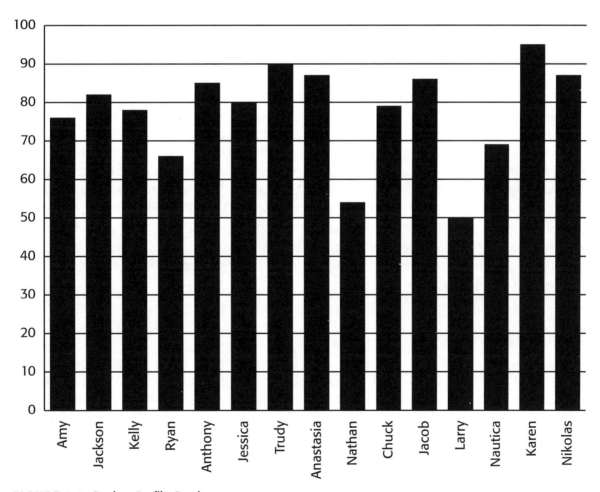

FIGURE 7.2 Student Profile Graph

intervention. This graph can also allow teachers to make sure student achievement and student ability match one another. Students should not have more than one deviation between their classroom grade and their short-cycle assessment results. In other words, if a student is receiving an A in your math class, he should not score any lower than a B on the math short-cycle assessment. If he does then his classroom achievement is not matching his ability, which is what the short-cycle assessment is supposed to measure. Similarly, if a student is getting a D in your language arts class, a red flag should go up if she receives a B on the reading short-cycle assessment. Somehow her ability is not coming out in her achievement in class. The student profile graph allows teachers to pinpoint any anomalies for the individual student.

Item Analysis Graph

The item analysis graph charts the questions themselves with the overall average of percentage correct for each question. The X axis represents each question identified by number, standard, and even format if the group so chooses. The Y axis represents the score of percent mastered. Since this is a mastery graph it is important to remember that on a one-point multiple choice question the student will need to get the question correct to earn mastery. At the same time, on a multi-point constructed response question the student will need to score at least 75% or 3 out of 4 on a 4-point question or 3 out of 3 on a 3-point question. Scoring 2 out of 4 on a 4-point question would only be a 50%—far from mastery. The same thing would apply to scoring 66% or 2 out of 3 on a 3-point question. Keep in mind the data is discerning mastery.

For an example, see Figure 7.3. To analyze the data on this particular graph you would look for the low-scoring questions and try to discern a pattern. In order to create your own item analysis graph, see the *Directions for Item Analysis Graph* and a blank *Item Analysis Graph*, in the Blueprints section, pages 131–132. You can break down the item analysis even further by looking at individual classes. Once again you are looking at overall patterns. If a majority of the students are having difficulty with a particular question, the cause could be a variety of things. That is what teachers will look at and figure out in their PLC.

Non-Mastery Report

To develop a non-mastery report, all you have to do is list each question and the names of students who did not master that particular question. A non-mastery report might look like Figure 7.4 on page 66. The non-mastery report will come in handy when dealing with instructional implications and the possible groupings of students. For your use we have included *Directions for Non-Mastery Report* and a blank template in the Blueprints section, pages 133–134. The organization of the data into these three reports

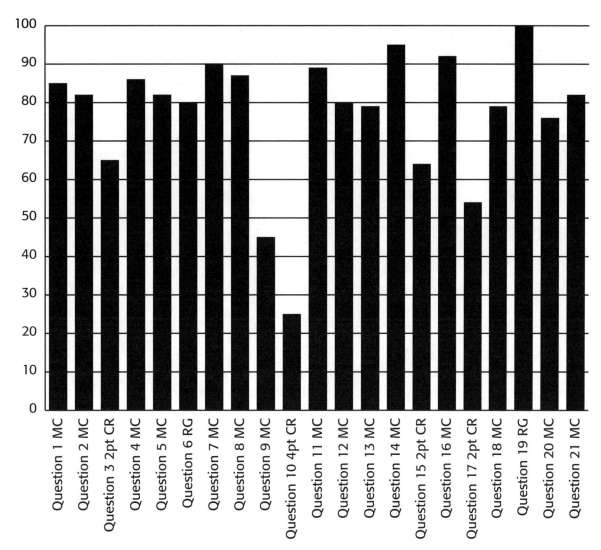

FIGURE 7.3 Item Analysis Graph

will give your PLC a good starting point for conversation. You can choose to spend one of your PLC meetings organizing the data, or have it prepared ahead of time so your group can begin to analyze it immediately.

Why Analyze as a PLC Group?

The advantages to analyzing the data in a group are the same as working within the PLC for every part of the SCORE Process: because two heads are better than one. It can be very difficult to look at our own classrooms and instructional strategies. We bring all the knowledge and baggage with us when looking at how students perform. In many

Question # 1, Standard 2-4
Multiply and divide fractions to solve problems.

Ryan
Nathan
Larry

Question #2, Standard 1-2
Round whole numbers and decimals to any place value.

Amy
Anastasia
Nikolas
Ryan
Larry

Question #3, Standard 6-3
Understand that probability can take any value between 0 and 1, where events that are not going to occur have a probability of 0, events certain to occur have a probability of 1, and more likely events have a higher probability than less likely events.

Anthony
Jessica
Ryan
Larry
Nautica
Chuck
Jacob
Kelly
Jackson

FIGURE 7.4 Non-Mastery Report

cases, knowing your students is a very good thing because you might be aware that a student suffers from test anxiety, or you might realize another student does not express herself well in written form. Either of these factors would explain poor results. The flip side of the coin is because we know our students so well, we can tend to not be as objective in our analysis as we need to be. We may show too much compassion instead of viewing the cold, hard analysis of the data as it stands. Sometimes we even can make excuses for our students, excuses that are not going to help them achieve higher results.

Working in a PLC to analyze the data allows others to give their input to student achievement as well. Being so close to things can sometimes lead to not seeing the forest through the trees. With so many eyes looking on, someone is bound to see the forest (most likely an East). Those very things that make the members of the group different from one another will help everyone see the entire picture. Remember, you cannot get anywhere with a compass that allows you to go in only one direction. You need to be able to go in all directions.

Leaving Your Ego at the Door

Looking at the data as a group can be a tough proposition because teachers are subjecting themselves to scrutiny. What if your class does not score as well as another class taking the same assessment? Does that mean you are not a good teacher? Some teachers in your PLC may feel this way. It is vital to establish a good rapport and level of comfort in your PLC group so that members are alright with having their data, warts and all, analyzed by the group The state test is supposed to make teachers accountable, and the assessment your PLC created should be no different. The difference here is that the accountability is being determined by a group of people you work with on a daily basis. These are professionals who are having their results looked at as well, rather than the faceless, nameless higher-ups in your state department who are looking at the results without knowing the individual students. This accountability is not to be used to judge teachers, but as evidence of adjustments that might need to be made in the classroom. These adjustments may be ones that were not visible before analyzing the data.

This is where the *norms* the PLC group created at the beginning of the process become very important. Teachers need to feel empowered to share their thoughts and ideas without worrying about hurting the feelings of a person whose data is not where he wants it to be. In order for the analysis of the data to work, it has to be honest without judgment. Putting someone down or blaming them is not something the PLC wants to do.

One problem associated with analyzing the data from the short-cycle assessments within the PLC sometimes lies in how it is said. One thing that helps with this is "we statements." In other words, instead of saying, "This is something you need to do," it is less threatening to phrase this as "This is something we need to do as a group or staff." That way, no one feels singled out or accused of doing a poor job. We teachers all want the same thing—success for our students.

PLC members need to enter the discussion of the data with an open mind. Although it can be very difficult, people need to be willing to hear things they may not want to in regard to their students. It is difficult not to take the results personally, but if the professional learning community approaches the data in a defensive manner, it will be very difficult to be open to change and professional growth. Everyone from the most veteran teacher to those fresh out of college need to be willing to adjust practices in the classroom if doing so is what is best for students.

How to Set Up Your Analysis

When you set up your PLC meetings regarding data analysis, there are a couple of methods that may be used. One is to suggest that everyone do their homework, analyzing their own class and looking for possible patterns. See the *Individual Assessment Reflection* list of questions to consider in the Blueprints section, page 135. Questions such as these could be asked of individual teachers:

◆ The students were most successful with which standard?
◆ The students had the most difficulty with which standard?
◆ Looking at individual students, were there capable students who did not do well? Please list them. Implications?
◆ Looking at individual students, were there less capable students who did better than you thought they would? Please list them. Implications?
◆ Were you satisfied overall with your classroom performance on this assessment? Explain.
◆ What could you do instructionally to improve your results for the next time?

By answering these questions, each member of the PLC will come to the meetings with information to share and compare. This will lay the groundwork for many of the conversations that will occur about what needs to be done for student success.

Another way is to have teachers come together and analyze the data as a group. When analyzing the results as a group, members will be looking for emerging patterns to explain success or areas for improvement. A worksheet, *Group Data Analysis for Assessment #1*, the PLC can use to guide them through the first assessment can be found in the Blueprints section on page 136. Questions the group might look at include these:

◆ What are the five most successful questions?
◆ What are the five least successful questions?
◆ What type of questions are the most and least successful questions (i.e., multiple choice, response grid, constructed response)?
◆ Are there standards or strands that repeat themselves in the most and least successful questions?
◆ What are the instructional implications of this information?

What will most likely emerge in the meeting concerning the first assessment is that students struggled with constructed response questions because students are not exposed to them. What will also come to the forefront are concerns about the assessment questions themselves. With the first assessment the PLC has written, there are bound to be snafus, mistakes, and misunderstandings that got in the way of students truly showing whether they understood the skill or not. It is important to note these in your PLC meetings and make revisions to the assessments accordingly, not to hold them against the students for not knowing those skills.

As the PLC ventures throughout the year using the SCORE Process, groups will find their needs, and areas of concern will shift as they get more comfortable with the process. We have included *Group Data Analysis* sheets for the entire year, each one slightly different in its intent and the possible impact on the classroom. You can find these in the Blueprints section pages 136–139. Use and alter these as the PLC sees fit.

What Might It Mean?

What all this conversation and data analysis means is if the results show students are not performing where they are expected to be, adjustments will need to be made in the classroom. How severe these adjustments are is dependent upon the findings of the PLC. One thing is very clear: You cannot expect change if nothing is changed. We will discuss the instructional implications that result from your PLC data analysis meetings in the next chapter.

If You Learn One Thing From This Chapter . . .

Organizing the data into useable information is important to the SCORE Process. There are three easy ways to organize the data:

1. Student Profile Graph
2. Item Analysis Graph
3. Non-Mastery Report

Each of these has its advantages. The student profile graph pinpoints issues with individual students, the item analysis graph looks at the assessment itself and possible gaps in the teaching process, and the non-mastery report gives a blueprint for how to reteach and the possibility of groupings.

The PLC will want to use the expertise it has in its group to both analyze the data and discern the next possible steps in the SCORE Process. In order for the discussion to be meaningful, members of the PLC need to be willing to be both open-minded and mindful of how they speak to others.

8

Adjustments in the Classroom

You will either step forward into growth or you will step back into safety.
                                                                    —Abraham Maslow

At this point in the SCORE Process, teachers have been working a lot on collaboration. They have been collaborating on aligning the standards, writing the assessments, and on grading and analyzing those same assessments. Throughout this entire time, teachers have been learning from one another, which is the point of working in a PLC. One of the biggest advantages of working on short-cycle assessments within a PLC is the help it provides in making adjustments in the classroom.

When working on this process by oneself, it can be difficult to figure out how to make adjustments. This is mostly because when working alone you are the only one providing feedback and observing your practices. The advantage of the PLC is offering teachers an outside view of their practices. This is somewhat like the armchair quarterback who sits back and can see all the flaws and opportunities missed. Members of the PLC can discover things individual teachers may not even be aware of. We have had groups that discovered such subtle things as teaching to one side of the classroom, or talking differently to boys than to girls. These are things a teacher might not discover without an additional set of eyes.

Data-Based Instructional Adjustments

Step 7 in the SCORE Process involves taking the information culled from the data analysis and making adjustments in the classroom. Notice we did not use the term *change*. If a person teaches primarily through lecture, he should not suddenly switch to hands-on learning. If a teacher employs project-based learning, she should not all of a sudden abandon this practice. In most cases, such widespread change is not needed. The SCORE Process calls for adjustments because these changes might be very slight, such as putting a learning objective for the week on the board, or phrasing some of the responses on unit tests as two- or three-part constructed responses rather than a long essay. There do not have to be major changes in order to make a difference, although in some cases radical thinking needs to be employed if radical change is what is desired.

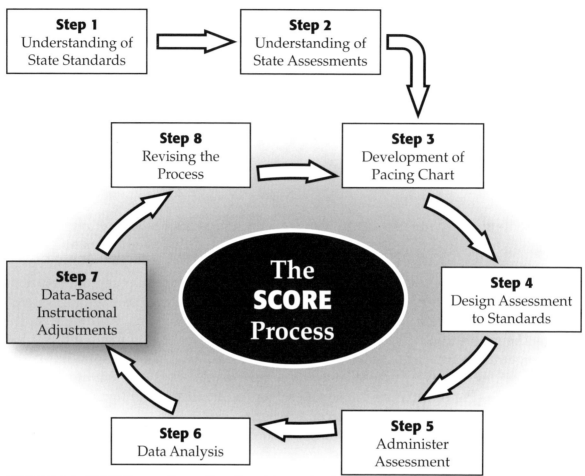

FIGURE 8.1 SCORE Process-Step 7: Data-Based Instructional Adjustments

Step 7: Data-Based Instructional Adjustments (Figure 8.1) is the SCORE Process stage at which the PLC is now. Notice that the instructional adjustments are data-based. The purpose of the PLC is not to require everyone to teach the same way using the same methods. The purpose is for teachers to see their own strengths and adjust accordingly. These adjustments should be made not just for the sake of making them, but because some pattern in the data indicates adjustments might be needed.

How to Use the Data to Make Adjustments

Using the data in the Student Profile Graph, the PLC can discern patterns much like a scientist would, to find answers to things that don't make sense. Let's take a look at the example Student Profile Graph from the previous chapter, Figure 8.2. Right away two students stand out immediately, Nathan and Larry. Both have scores right around 50%. So as a PLC you may begin by looking at them. Are these typically poorly performing students who have difficulty showing mastery of standards in regular classroom practices? If so, what intervention plan has been put into place to help these two achieve mastery? If intervention plans are already in motion, this information might just reflect typical classroom performance. Or, this information might suggest the modifications and accommodations already in place are not adequate. This might also indicate communication between the regular classroom teacher and the special educator (if one is involved) needs to be stronger.

When looking at individual students who did not perform well on the short-cycle assessment according to the Student Profile Graph, you might want to keep learning styles in mind. Perhaps the student's preferred mode of learning is kinesthetic, while the assessment requires strong visual skills. This is important to know if you are going to make adjustments to instruction. Giving each student a learning inventory is a good way to differentiate instruction if you think some students have not been able to learn what has been taught for the assessments. There are several different types of learning style profiles or inventories, and many are readily available on the Internet. For your

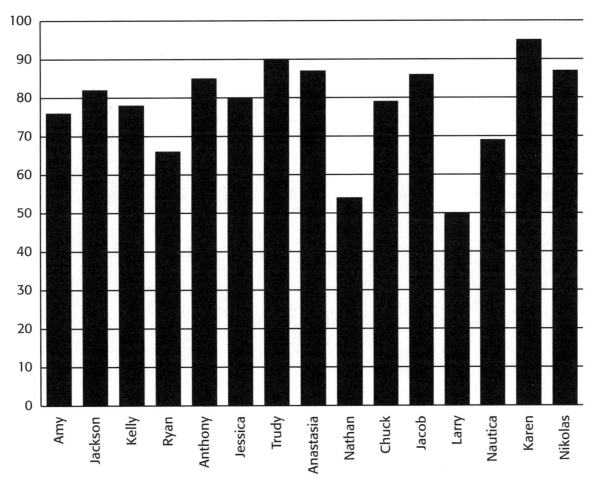

FIGURE 8.2 Student Profile Graph

convenience, we have provided an example of a *Learning Style Inventory* in the Blue-prints section, page 140.

Let's imagine, however, Larry is normally a very strong student, pulling down B's in class. The question becomes, why the poor performance on the assessment? If a student performs poorly in comparison to his achievement, there could be several factors involved:

- ◆ The student may suffer from text anxiety.
- ◆ The student may have bubbled in the wrong number once, throwing the entire sequence off.
- ◆ The student may be a poor writer as reflected in the constructed response questions, pulling down the overall results.
- ◆ The student may be a hard worker who achieves high grades because of work habits and not ability.
- ◆ The student may not have been feeling well the day of the assessment or forgot to have breakfast and was feeling lightheaded.
- ◆ The student may learn best through a different learning modality than the testing situation employs.

These are all possible roads of investigation to pursue as a reason for an unexpected poor performance on a short-cycle assessment. To help you determine the cause of poor performance we have provided you with a checklist called a *Short-Cycle Assessment Performance Causal Checklist* on page 143 in the Blueprints section.

Some red flags, on the other hand, may occur for students who performed well but who typically are not strong students. Let's take Anthony who scored above an 80%, yet is failing your class. There are several factors to consider for a student showing ability on assessments while not showing the same ability in the classroom. Some of these factors are:

- ◆ The student does not do his homework regularly which pulls his grades down.
- ◆ The student's attendance or behavior causes a lower grade.
- ◆ The student is embarrassed socially to do well in class so he underachieves.
- ◆ The student has a poor home life that may prevent him from reaching his potential.
- ◆ The student might have gotten lucky.

Again, these factors can be found in the causal checklist. Always keep in mind that, like any good scientist, you will need to investigate the reason behind these differences. That is what analysis involves.

The Student Profile Graph will provide specific areas of adjustments with individual students. The Item Analysis Graph, on the other hand, looks at the class overall as well as the assessment itself. Let's take the Item Analysis Graph from the previous

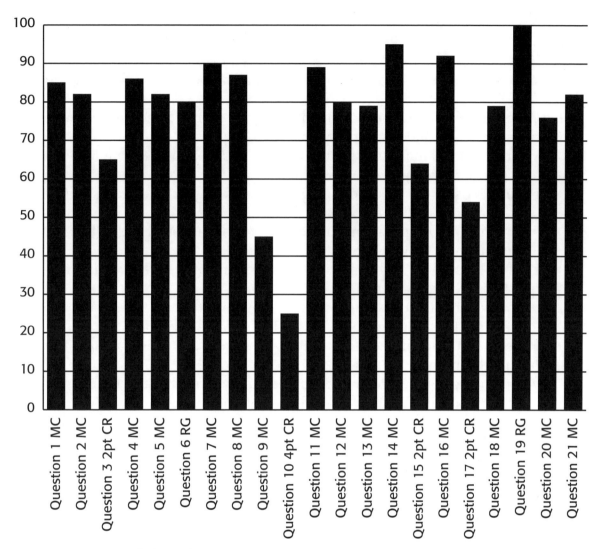

FIGURE 8.3 Item Analysis Graph

chapter, Figure 8.3. What the PLC should look for in a graph such as this are patterns and instructional implications related to them. For instance, notice four out of the five lowest scores are questions 3, 10, 15, and 17, all constructed response questions. The obvious question is, "Are students missing the question because of the content, or because of the format?" The pattern here seems to indicate format since none of the constructed response questions were mastered.

Question 9 is also a low-scoring question. It is important to figure out as a PLC whether this occurs as a result of the students not understanding the content or not understanding the question. It could be that the question was unclear and may need to be rewritten. If it is the content, what actions need to be made to make sure students are retaught or given another opportunity to show they can master the skill?

In looking at successful questions, question 19 is the highest on the item analysis graph. This may mean the PLC teachers did a good job of teaching that skill. Remember it is just as important to look at successes as it is areas of improvement.

Here are some patterns to consider when looking at the Item Analysis Graph:

◆ Pattern: Most of the lower scoring questions are constructed response questions for which students have to write their responses.
  • Instructional implication: Students need more exposure to multipart questions and writing in the classroom.
◆ Pattern: Most of the lower scoring questions are higher level standards (according to your Taxonomy Table).
  • Instructional implication: Students need more exposure to higher level questions in the classroom.
◆ Pattern: Most of the higher scoring questions are lower level, multiple choice questions (according to your Taxonomy Table).
  • Instructional implication: Continue to expose students to these because they are the building blocks for the higher level questions.
◆ Pattern: Lower scoring questions are coming from the same standard category (i.e., math—probability).
  • Instructional implication: This may be a standard that as a teaching staff is not instructionally strong. We all have strengths and weaknesses as teachers. The key is to improve areas of weakness through professional development or collaboration.
◆ Pattern: Higher scoring questions are coming from the same standard category (i.e., math—patterns).
  • Instructional implication: This may be a standard that is taught often in whatever textbook/materials are used. You may need to adjust the amount of time you spend on this standard, as it may be taking time away from a standard with which your students have more difficulty.
◆ Pattern: Students start out strong with higher mastery at the beginning questions, but sort of fade toward the last few questions.
  • Instructional implication: Students need to work on one of two things or maybe both: a) endurance in sitting and taking a test, giving the same effort at the end of the test as the beginning, and b) pacing their time when taking the test; they may have run out of time and left a few of the questions at the end blank.

Sometimes you won't see an overall pattern in the data, but just isolated questions on which students do poorly. There could be many reasons for this:

◆ The standard wasn't taught by everyone either because of running out of time or unforeseen circumstances such as weather days or too many assemblies.
◆ The standard wasn't taught at the level it needed to be in all classes because students took longer to grasp it at a lower level.

- ♦ It is a difficult standard to understand and it needs to continue to be revisited.
- ♦ The language of the questions, although mirroring those used by the state assessment, was confusing to the students.
- ♦ The answer key was incorrect.
- ♦ The question wasn't very clear and students misunderstood it or a typo caused them to misunderstand the question.

Any of the first four reasons listed for poor performance would suggest that adjustments are needed in the classroom.

If the reason for a poor performance is one of the latter two listed, there may need to be revisions to the assessment itself. To help you keep track of revisions following administration, we have provided a *Post Assessment Revision Form* on page 145 of the Blueprints. We strongly urge that you simply list the possible revisions in the PLC meeting following the administration of the short-cycle assessment. It is easy to get caught up in rewriting the questions (especially if the students did not do well) instead of looking at the instruction that led up to the assessment. If you list the problem questions, along with your concerns or suggestions, you will be able to easily go back and address these revisions in a later PLC meeting.

Many times the item analysis graph will indicate those questions that may need to be revised because they are not clear or have mistakes. You should not revise a question to make it easier even if a majority of the students missed it. If you feel the urge to do this, remember to ask yourself if the question is truly fair and meets the standard. If you decide it is, examine how the standard was taught. Many times we as teachers want to change the question rather than instruction.

Grouping of Students

The non-mastery report will help with the grouping of students for differentiated instruction. It lists for teachers all those students who did not master a certain standard, indicating these students may need to be retaught the concept.

See Figure 8.4, the non-mastery report, which was discussed in the previous chapter. This report enables you to determine flexible grouping for differentiated instruction. If you see that nine students missed question 3, and the PLC group determines the standard needs to be retaught to these students, you can group those students together without having to drag in all the other students who mastered that particular standard. At the same time, a question—under which the names of most of the class appear—would demonstrate the need to reteach that standard to the whole class.

The non-mastery report gives you a good idea where you need to differentiate instruction without creating permanent groups. It is valuable to have flexible grouping in the classroom not only to move students at different levels, but to place emphasis on different areas according to student need. Just because someone is an A student does not mean she understands everything and, on the flip side, just because someone is

Question # 1, Standard 2-4
Multiply and divide fractions to solve problems.

Ryan
Nathan
Larry

Question #2, Standard 1-2
Round whole numbers and decimals to any place value.

Amy
Anastasia
Nikolas
Ryan
Larry

Question #3, Standard 6-3
Understand that probability can take any value between 0 and 1, where events that are not going to occur have a probability of 0, events certain to occur have a probability of 1, and more likely events have a higher probability than less likely events.

Anthony
Jessica
Ryan
Larry
Nautica
Chuck
Jacob
Kelly
Jackson

FIGURE 8.4 Non-Mastery Report

failing your class does not mean he is not mastering certain skills. To help you organize your flexible groups and determine differentiated instructional strategies, we have provided a tool, *Differentiated Instruction Flexible Groups*, in the Blueprints section on page 147.

Flexible grouping may mean a completely different way to think about grouping students not just in your classroom, but in the school. Since this work is being done as a PLC, this could be an opportunity to institute schoolwide adjustments. For example, if there is a group of twenty-five 7th graders all struggling with a particular standard according to the non-mastery report but who are difficult to schedule together because they come from four different classes, what's to say you can't group those students together in order to reteach the concept? For those forward-thinking PLC groups, the non-mastery report might allow them to determine tutoring groups, math intervention classes, students who need to get some additional work with computer practice skills for a particular subject area, or other such groupings. We once worked with a school district that created study groups run by teachers for the last hour of the school day. How they determined where to place students was based on the non-mastery list. Some students might be assigned to a study group run by the math teacher because the students had difficulty with questions concerning algebra, while another group went to the English teacher for a deficiency in writing skills. The entire school was involved in the grouping and students were placed where they would best receive help on what they did not master. Students who had mastered certain skills or standards were able to be a part of groups where they were encouraged to delve deeper into the content, thus eliminating boredom and ensuring growth for all students. When schools use PLCs to analyze the data from short-cycle assessments, this means not only are conversations happening as a community, but instructional implications are as well.

Chances for Collaboration

When analyzing data in your PLC group, it is important to look not just at the students overall, but individual classes as well. This might show a couple of things; one, which classrooms may need adjustments, and two, which teachers are having great success. Because you are working in a professional learning community this is the best chance you are going to have to engage in collaboration with other teachers. This can be something as small as how you set up your classroom or as large as revamping your method of teaching.

Looking at this data will be one of the best opportunities to participate in teacher collaboration. For instance, if a teacher is having difficulty with a particular standard, he might ask other teachers instructing the same standard with better success what they are doing. This could mean an exchange of lesson plans, a classroom observation, the borrowing of a book, or other such professional development. Similarly, if a teacher is having great success with a standard as evidenced by the data, this would be the time to pick her brain and determine what she is doing to garner such results. Maybe she has a lesson, technique, or strategy she can share with the group that will help in teaching that same standard.

Working within a PLC will allow for conversations to learn from one another as teachers. One of the biggest complaints in the teaching community seems to be that we are not given enough time to sit down and share ideas. A PLC provides this chance, so make sure to take full advantage of it.

If You Learn One Thing From This Chapter...

Adjustments must be made in the classroom in order for there to be a change in student achievement. Doing the same thing over and over again and expecting different results is not a very realistic approach.

Teachers in the professional learning community can use the various reports, the student profile graph, the item analysis graph, and the non-mastery report to identify patterns and pinpoint possible adjustments in individual classes as well as throughout the school. The PLC can discuss these possible adjustments and how they will help students attain higher achievement.

It is important not to forget one of the richest resources available for possible adjustments in teaching practices—each other. Your PLC has a plethora of perspectives, ideas, and teaching techniques within it. It would behoove your group to take advantage of this valuable resource and mine it for everything it has to offer.

9

Keeping Up With Collaboration

Good design begins with honesty, asks tough questions, comes from collaboration and from trusting your intuition.

—Freemason Thomas

There will be many chances for collaboration in the conversations the professional learning community will engage in throughout the process. While discussing difficult standards to teach, a science teacher might share an interesting lesson regarding the refraction of light and the use of mirrors. While writing a question for an assessment, an English teacher might share how she has her students break down three part constructive response questions and code them for better understanding. While analyzing the data from the assessment, the group might discover the math teacher has a very effective way to teach the quadratic formula that hadn't been considered before.

Many times this collaboration will come as a result of simply having a group of teachers in the same room. There will be other times when the collaboration needs to be a bit more deliberate. This does not mean forcing the collaboration, but rather making the opportunity available as a PLC. Whether individuals decide to take advantage of this or not is completely up to them.

Revising the Process

This brings us to Step 8 in the SCORE Process, revising the process. Since your PLC will be giving a series of formative short-cycle assessments over the course of the school year, the process it went through in order to write the first assessment will repeat itself as many times as there are assessments. Some of the SCORE steps will be reviewed quickly such as understanding the standards and the state assessment. There may have to be a discussion concerning a particularly complex or confusing standard giving students difficulty, but this will most likely not be as time consuming as it was in the beginning.

Of course the group will go through the steps of designing the assessment, refining procedures in the administration, analyzing the data, and making instructional adjustments. One thing not to forget is revising what didn't work in the past assessment. That is what Step 8 is all about. (See Figure 9.1.) The Pacing Chart will need to be reviewed. Was the group able to teach the required standards in a manner with which they felt comfortable? Did the students master the standards? Can the mastery of the standards be backed up with data? If not, certain standards might have to be moved, reassessed, or approached in a different manner. Remember we said from the beginning that the Pacing Chart is not written in stone. It is a living, breathing document that will need to be changed from time to time.

Revisiting Assessments

It is strongly recommended the PLC get together for a meeting after all the data have been sifted through and instructional implications figured out, in order to revise the assessment just given. This is done for a couple of reasons. First, using the group's item

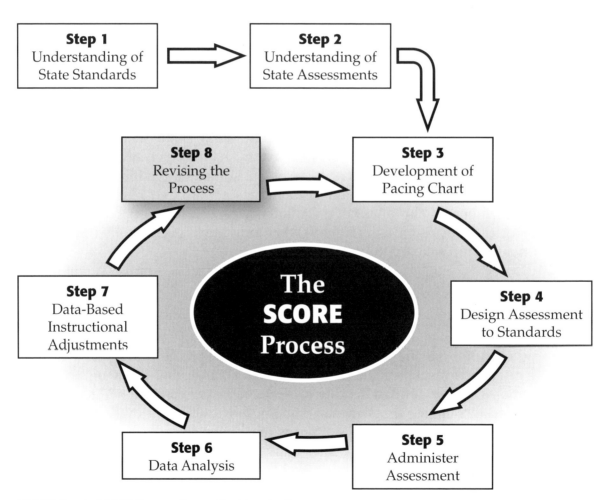

FIGURE 9.1 SCORE Process-Step 8: Revising the Process

analysis data, every question the students had difficulty with should be revisited to make sure it is written as clearly as the PLC wants it to be. This does not mean changing questions to make them easier. It means determining whether the skill the Pacing Chart wishes to assess is truly being measured. For example, if a standard is supposed to be challenging students at a synthesis level, the PLC will want to make sure the question indeed does that. The PLC will also want to revisit questions students scored very highly on to make sure the distracters are not too easy or the question is asked at a level lower than it should be.

The problem with waiting until the next year to pull out the assessment and revising it is that the issues that were fresh in the group's minds become dull with time and may be forgotten. This is where the Post Assessment Revision Form introduced in the previous chapter is an essential tool to use immediately after giving each assessment. This tool can be used to capture possible revisions to the assessment while they are still on everyone's mind.

To collect additional information about the assessment and the procedures for administering it, the PLC might even want to consider informally or formally surveying the students. Teachers ask general questions of their students or have students fill out formal surveys to gather feedback. Some of this information may be useful in creating the testing environment the next time, but also might expose additional areas teachers need to work on with students. For a sample teachers can use see the *Student Questionnaire* in the Blueprints section, page 149.

Celebrate Your Success

One thing we sometimes forget to do in education is celebrate our successes. After the first assessment, it is important to let students know that doing well is valued, not just because they got a good result, but the school and teachers appreciate their success. It will also help students to see the value in the SCORE Process and not view it as being tested to death. This will go far in helping to establish a positive attitude for the next round of short-cycle assessments.

These celebrations can be as grand or as subtle as the PLC chooses. An example of something grand would be having a school assembly where top students are given certificates for their achievements. As the process goes along, you can add most "improved student" and "steadiest student." Recognition can also come in the form of morning announcements where names of high achievers are given over the speakers. In subtle ways each teacher can decide how to celebrate success. A teacher might create a top-five achievement chart he displays in his classroom. A teacher may display the student profile, minus names, highlighting those students with highest scores. She may also display the item analysis and trumpet those standards the students mastered at a high percentage.

However the school decides to celebrate, as individual teachers or as a collective school, doing so will work wonders in improving the student and teacher attitude toward the testing.

Classroom Visits

Once the assessment has been revised and celebrated, it is critical to continue to foster the idea of collaboration within your PLC group. There are various ways to do this, one being classroom visits. Seeing is believing. This is an important axiom when it comes to professional development in general. Many times teachers attend a conference where there is a guest speaker who talks at the audience about what can be done to improve achievement in the classroom. No matter the reputation of this speaker, there is no substitute for seeing best practices unfold in the classroom itself. Having the time to actually see your colleagues as they work with students in the classroom is a very valuable practice in which all teachers should engage. Even catching 15 to 20 minutes of a lesson will provide the possibility of several ideas a teacher can take and adopt in her classroom. Seeing the reactions of the students, the dynamic of the classroom and teacher, as well as the adjustments when roadblocks to learning are encountered, is an invaluable experience.

These observations do not need to be teachers of your same grade and subject area to be valuable. A math teacher might learn a lot about classroom management by watching a gym teacher. A social studies teacher might get some excellent ideas of how to teach nonfiction by observing a language arts teacher. A science teacher might get some excellent ideas for how to set up work stations by seeing them in action in a music or art class.

The issue in this case is time; how are classroom visits coordinated in order to make them meaningful? It would be nice if teachers were simply empowered to make these efforts on their own and learn from the experiences. The reality is some teachers may need a little guidance in this matter. What we find most effective is to have a clear plan in place for such a professional development effort. An example would be for teachers to set up three classroom observations in a month's time.

1. Classroom of same subject area
2. Classroom of same grade level
3. Classroom of neither subject area or grade level.

These observations can be made during a planning period. Another idea would be to have a curriculum person or substitute teacher cover the classes of those who want to observe. To help with the planning of the observations, we have included the *Observation Planning and Reflection Tool* in the Blueprints section on page 151. It might also be good to post a master schedule of who is observing who at what time and where so there is no doubling up. This will also ensure that some teachers aren't getting multiple observers while others are receiving none, as well as making accountable those teachers who have not yet made observations. To that end, we have included a *Master Observation Schedule* on page 152 in the Blueprints section.

We do realize sometimes schedules are impossible to work around and observations may be difficult to make. If this is the case, teachers could videotape lessons they wish to share with others to create a community collection of lessons that people can take with them and watch when their schedule allows it.

Once the month is up, teachers should get together in their PLC meeting and discuss what was observed, sharing what was seen and how they might incorporate strategies and lessons into their own classrooms. This will give the group plenty of fodder for rich discussion

Sharing Best Practices

Another method for collaboration is to allow for best practices to be shared by teachers. A best practice is a technique, a lesson, or a philosophy a teacher feels is a strength of hers and would be beneficial to share with others. This could be something the teacher read about in a book or article, learned at a conference, picked up online, observed from another teacher, or just something she developed on her own. The sharing of best practices can be done in a number of ways.

- ◆ Ask a teacher in the building to share a best practice with the entire group, using hands-on examples where appropriate.
- ◆ Invite an outside speaker or expert to share a best practice. Make sure it is someone who will share useful classroom practices rather than just theory.
- ◆ Break into smaller groups and have a person in each group prepare a best practice to share. The groups can then report out so that many of the practices are heard.
- ◆ Have everyone come ready to share a best practice, then go around the circle sharing a 5-minute summary of a practice to give teachers a flavor of it.
- ◆ Have a teaching team present a best practice their team developed.
- ◆ Present an article from an educational review that shares a best practice, conducting a roundtable discussion concerning it and the implications for specific classrooms.
- ◆ Have the curriculum coordinator or leader of the PLC choose a best practice she thinks will address an issue that came from the data the first assessment provided, using it to create an overall strategy the PLC will employ for higher student achievement.

One important thing to remember is to give the sharer uninterrupted time in which he lays out the information. The teachers listening should record their questions as the presentation is going on, and time should be built in at the end to address these. We have provided a *Best Practice Sharing Chart* in the Blueprints section, page 153 to help organize thoughts and questions during the sharing time.

However you choose to do it, sharing best practices is a great way for collaboration to occur and for adjustments to happen in the classroom. Even if these are not adjustments made as a result of the data analysis, the end result will be better teaching practices and, ultimately, higher student achievement.

Forming a Critical Friends Group

Your PLC groups might transform into a Critical Friends Group (CFG). In a CFG teachers get together to discuss dilemmas, look at student work and lesson plans, share best practices, and collaborate with one another to improve classroom practices. A CFG purposely uses protocols in order to facilitate the group and lead them through issues that come up in the day-to-day teaching of students. A list of protocols can be found at the School Reform Initiative website (http://www.schoolreforminitiative.org).

Scheduling Future Meetings for Assessments 1–4

Figure 9.2 is an example of what the schedule for the SCORE Process might look like for the first assessment. There is a balance of before and after school meetings as well as early release days to work on the big projects such as writing the assessment and the data analysis. This seems like a lot of meetings, but keep in mind there will not need to be as much time spent in subsequent assessments. See Figure 9.3, the second assessment schedule. Notice when working on Assessment 2, four meetings have been eliminated by the combination of steps while other meetings have been shortened as a result of previous work. Figure 9.4 shows an example of the third and fourth 9-week assessments PLC meeting schedules. When working through the SCORE Process for Assessment 3 and 4, the PLC group is down to four meetings. Teachers have become familiar enough with the process and understand it to the point they do not need a full meeting to go over the directions for administering, or they can combine activities such as looking at the Pacing Chart and writing the assessment.

Does that mean the PLC should not meet as often? That is up to the group. You certainly do not want to burn out anyone on the process, but at the same time you don't want to have too few meetings so that the teachers get out of practice. Even scheduling short meetings where everyone gets together to make sure they are still on the same page can be effective in maintaining your professional learning community. To help you plan for your PLC meetings we have provided you with a blank *Meeting Schedule* in the Blueprints section, page 154.

Meeting	Type/Length of Meeting	Topic
1	Preschool work day	Introductions/Identifying various group styles
2	Preschool work day	Step 1 of the SCORE Process: Understanding the State Standards
3	After school meeting 2 hours	Step 2 of the SCORE Process: Understanding the State Assessment
4	Before school meeting 2 hours	Step 3 of the SCORE Process: The Pacing Chart
5	Half-day release	Step 4 of the SCORE Process: Writing the Assessment
6	After-school meeting 1 hour	Step 5 of the SCORE Process: Directions for Administration
7	After-school meeting 2 hours	Grading of the Assessments
8	Half day release	Steps 6 and 7 of the SCORE Process: Data Analysis and Instructional Implications
9	After-school meeting 2 hours	Continuation of Step 7 of the SCORE Process: Instructional Implications
10	Before-school meeting 1 hour	Step 8 of the SCORE Process: Revising the Process/Best Practices

FIGURE 9.2 Assessment 1

Meeting	Type/Length of Meeting	Topic
1	Preschool work day 1 hour	Revisit Steps 1, 2 and 3 of the SCORE Process: Understanding the State Standards, Understanding the State Assessments and the Pacing Chart
2	Half-day release	Step 4 of the SCORE Process: Writing the Assessment
3	After-school meeting ½ hour	Step 5 of the SCORE Process: Administering the Assessment
4	After-school meeting 2 hours	Grading of the Assessments
5	Half-day release	Steps 6 and 7 of the SCORE Process: Data Analysis and Instructional Implications
6	Before-school meeting 1 hour	Step 8 of the SCORE Process: Revising the Process/Best Practices

FIGURE 9.3 Assessment 2

Meeting Even When Nothing Is Wrong

We teachers tend to get into the habit of meeting only when something is wrong. Too often the philosophy is "don't fix it unless it's broken." However, once something is broken it might already be too late, or we might not even be aware it is broken until the damage is done. A good habit is to meet in your PLC even when a meeting doesn't seem to be warranted. Take advantage of time spent together, sharing best practices, reporting what is going on in the classroom, and celebrating individual successes.

Teachers often complain they do not know what is going on in the classroom right next to theirs because of the isolation teaching can foster. This is the time to share what

Meeting	Type/Length of Meeting	Topic
1	Half-day release	Revisit Step 3 of the SCORE Process: the Pacing Chart and complete Step 4: Writing the Assessment
	Sent in an email	Additions to Step 5 of the SCORE Process: Administering the Assessment
2	After-school meeting 2 hours	Grading of the Assessments
3	Half-day release	Steps 6 and 7 of the SCORE Process: Data Analysis and Instructional Implications
4	Before-school meeting 1 hour	Step 8 of the SCORE Process: Revising the Process/Best Practices

FIGURE 9.4 Assessment 3

is going on in your classroom. Use these meetings to work on the morale and dynamics of the PLC, as these need to be fostered constantly and consistently throughout the year. Even during the summer when the greatest gap of time apart occurs, have a summer retreat or even a social event such as a barbeque. Activities like this are simple enough to set up and go a long way in maintaining the good will of the group.

If You Learn One Thing From This Chapter . . .

Collaborating is like a stew—you have to keep it simmering and add the proper ingredients, tending to it carefully, otherwise you'll end up with mush. Collaboration is not something that just happens: it must be deliberate and planned. Things the PLC can do to elicit collaboration are classroom visits, sharing of best practices, and revising the SCORE Process. This sharing of ideas will make the members of your PLC better teachers and will result in higher student achievement.

Epilogue

Teamwork is the ability to work together toward a common vision. The ability to direct individual accomplishments toward organizational objectives. It is the fuel that allows common people to attain uncommon results.

—Andrew Carnegie

The reason for writing this book using the SCORE Process, which was already outlined in our first book, *Short-Cycle Assessments: Improving Student Achievement through Formative Assessment* (Lang, Stanley, & Moore, 2008), is because of the value of working through the process within a professional learning community. Having worked with thousands of teachers in over 50 districts, we have seen good collaboration and poor collaboration. When collaboration fails, it is usually due to such simple things as organization, a handful of poor attitudes, or impatient administrators not willing to give the process the couple of years it takes to garner huge results. Where we see the biggest breakdowns are when people are not willing to work with one another or take the time to learn how to work with others.

When the process works, as it does in most cases, it is really powerful. The schools in which we saw the largest success were those where teachers were in small professional learning communities, working toward a common goal, and achieved high student success through collective efforts. We know PLCs are the best way to unfold the SCORE Process, but we also know it isn't simply a matter of throwing a bunch of teachers together into the deep end of a pool and seeing if they can all swim. Like most good things, this process must be designed well. This is why we thought a book focused on how to plan out a short-cycle assessment process within a PLC would be beneficial to teachers.

Now that you have gone through the process, our last bit of advice is something we call the four Ps:

♦ Patience
♦ Planning
♦ Prudence
♦ Patience

Patience comes in the form of learning to work with one another, trusting everyone has everyone's best interest, and more important, the best interest of the students. Working with a group is far more difficult than working individually in that you have to take time for discussion and compromise. Undoubtedly the group will produce better work than someone working by himself. Why do you think we write these books as a team? It is because one person's weakness is another's strength. Any idea forgotten or left out is caught by the other, or new things the other has learned is shared between us. We are practicing what we preach.

Planning is valuable in that organizing so many voices in so many tasks involves good planning. How well it is organized will make or break your PLC group. Teachers have enough constraints to deal with without having to worry about disorganization and wasting time. We have shown you many ways to be deliberate about this; don't take this aspect lightly.

Prudence comes in the form of working through the process correctly and carefully. Every corner the group cuts to make things easier simply makes things more difficult in the end. There's a reason for the saying, "Whatever is worth doing is worth doing well." Think about your students and what you expect of them. Do you want them to do work for the sake of doing work, or do you want them to put forth their best effort so they are learning from it? Teachers should expect the same of themselves.

Finally there is *Patience* again. This is not a typo. Your PLC will need extra patience. There will be times when the process seems impossible and people will want to give it up to try something else. This is where patience plays its largest role. If you are patient with the process and see it through, doing a high quality job, you will see results. Of this we are sure.

Blueprints for the Process

These reproducibles should aid you in your journey to create formative short-cycle assessments within your professional learning community.

Advantages/Disadvantages of PLC Groups

	Team	Grade Level	School	District	Multidistrict
Advantages	• Puts a small group of people on the same page. • Easy to manage. • Would be easier to find a common planning time. • Will reach a larger number of students than a single teacher would.	• Puts everyone in a common grade on the same page. • Allows collaboration between teachers who teach the same subject and grade level. • Allows consistency between all teachers in a grade level.	• Puts everyone on the same page in the school. • Vertical alignment between grades is much smoother. • Allows for lots of collaboration because everyone is involved and sharing ideas. • Many teachers receiving professional development at one time.	• Puts everyone on the same page in the district. • Vertical alignment between buildings is easier. • Affects a greater number of people, allowing for quicker transformation. • Students moving from building to building will still be familiar with the format and structure.	• Puts everyone on the same page in many districts. • Affects a very large number of people. • Allows students switching districts to have an easier transition. • Provides many voices for collaboration.
Disadvantages	• Only affects the people on the team, a limited number (2–5 teachers). • Allows limited collaboration since teachers teach different subjects.	• Only affects the teachers on that grade level (5–10 teachers). • Can be challenging to find time for the group to meet.	• In order to have common planning to work in groups the staff will have to organize times before or after school, or an in-service day. • Has a bigger risk of dissenting teachers causing problems.	• Could be difficult to coordinate schedule of different buildings that get out at different times. • Organizing such a large group could present a challenge.	• Organizing common time could be a challenge considering coordination may have to take into account several different schedules. • Even finding a common space could provide a challenge. • Could be a challenge to get so many people to compromise.

Forming Norms

Materials:
- ♦ sticky notes
- ♦ chart paper/whiteboard
- ♦ pens

Roles:
- ♦ scribe
- ♦ spokesperson
- ♦ moderator

Step 1: Give each person a dozen or so sticky notes and a pen. Propose the following: "What do you need in order to work effectively in a group?"

Step 2: Allow people 5 to 10 minutes to write down ideas. Make sure they know to put one idea per sticky note.

Step 3: Once it appears everyone has finished, invite them to come up to the whiteboard/chart paper and cluster similar ideas together.

Step 4: Select a spokesperson to come to the board and read the ideas.

Step 5: As each idea is shared, the moderator leads a group discussion, making sure everyone agrees to the idea or getting more information as to why the person who suggested it did so. If everyone agrees it is a valid idea, it is crafted into a concise norm.

Step 6: Select a scribe to write on a piece of paper or a piece of butcher paper the ideas that are agreed on.

Step 7: Someone will eventually need to type the norms up and provide copies for everyone.

Icebreaker Activities

Here are some icebreakers that can be used to begin a meeting:

- ◆ Give a penny to everyone. Have them look at the date on the penny and talk about something significant that happened to them that year.
- ◆ Have people describe the details of their ideal, perfect vacation.
- ◆ Place a piece of paper and markers on a table. Have people draw their ideal classroom including equipment, setup, etc.
- ◆ Have participants mingle with one another and try to identify the person whose birthday is closest to theirs. Then find out 3 things they have in common and share this with the group.
- ◆ Have group members say 3 things about themselves, 2 true and 1 false. Everyone else then tries to guess which the false statement is.
- ◆ On an index card have participants answer the following questions: favorite color, animal, TV show, hobby, and food. Someone mixes all the cards together and reads them aloud. The group tries to guess to whom the card belongs.
- ◆ As each person enters the room, place an index card on their back with the name of a celebrity. The person must move around the room, asking others yes or no questions to try and figure out the famous person on their index card.
- ◆ Have participants play personal bingo. Each participant will make a bingo sheet with things such as "likes Chinese food," "has traveled to another country," "has never been to a funeral." Go around the room and find a different person for each square until you have bingo.

Ice Breaker Bingo

Find people in the room who fit the description.
Try and get four spots in a row in order to win.

Likes Chinese food	Has both a dog and a cat at home	Has been to a professional football game	Has met a celebrity in person
Can say hello in 3 languages	Can rub tummy and pat head at same time	Has ridden a bike in the last week	Is wearing something black
Can say the alphabet backwards	Knows all fifty state capitals	Can whistle	Has a middle name with 3 syllables
Has seen the movie _____	Is chewing gum	Can name all 6 children on Brady Bunch	Has flown on an airplane this year

Compass Points

NORTH
"Action"
"Get it done"

WEST
"Details"
"Organization"
"Scheduler"

EAST
"Study"
"Analyze"
"Think about it"

SOUTH
"People person"
"Everyone feels heard"
"Make sure everyone is one board"

1. What adjectives would you use to describe strengths for your compass direction?

2. What adjectives would you use to describe weaknesses for your compass direction?

3. Which compass direction do you think you would work best with? Which would be the most challenging?

4. If your team did not have your compass direction, how do you think it would function?

Profile of a Student

Developed by Gene Thompson-Grove for National School Reform Faculty (NSRF;2008)

Student 1

You are life smart, but not school smart. You would do almost anything to not look stupid in school. You are the class clown, or the loud political protester, or the persistent talker—on the edge of being a "behavior problem." You don't mind being sent to the office instead of having to give an oral presentation—and you know just how to get sent there. Everyone at the office knows you well and greets you with affection, as they know you as "really, a nice kid." The things you are really good at seem to have little place in school.

Student 2

You are a good but unremarkable student. You have figured out what each of your teachers wants, and you do exactly that—on time, and completely. You are a committed student, but take few risks, and so seldom challenge yourself to higher levels of learning. You are one of those kids people talk about—the quiet kid whose work always falls within the "norm." Because you complete your work, get A's and B's, and are never any trouble, you are often overlooked.

Student 3

You love learning. You can't get enough of it. You actually look up those books that your teachers mention in passing and independently figure out alternative math theorems—just for fun. Your only beef with school is the busy work you have to do and those classes you have to take with kids who just don't seem to care about learning.

Student 4

Who are you anyway? It often takes teachers a full semester to remember your name, and you often feel invisible. This is either because you like it that way [i.e., you sit in the back and hide behind textbooks, hats, whatever—happily forgoing a few percentages to keep from going public, and doing decent but unremarkable work to keep a low profile]. Or, this is because you feel disenfranchised and disempowered, for all kinds of reasons. You watch the "in" students with a mixture of envy and disdain. You know more about certain subjects than they do, but most teachers don't know that.

Student 5

In your mind, there is no way you can succeed in school. You have been a "remedial" student from before your memory kicked in. You read slowly and seldom get a passing grade on an in-class essay. You do have strengths, but no one seems to notice or value those. You wonder if life after high school will feel like more of the same.

Student 6

You are a finely tuned teacher-pleasing machine. You know exactly what you need to do to maximize your grade and you do it (no matter what) and then some. You are organized, disciplined, and focused—on your homework, on getting good grades, and on your extra curricular activities, which will look good on your transcript when you apply to college. Your teachers know you will always volunteer for anything they ask—and you often do.

Student 7

You are an efficiency hound so you can have time for other things in your life—the lowest passing grade possible for the least amount of work is your mantra. Why pass a class with a 78% when you can pass with a 69.2% and a good sob story? You know all the tricks: make up tests, rewrites, re-dos, extra credit points, parental pressure, coach pressure, group work (with the right partners). You put more effort into beating the game than learning.

Student 8

You have a creative mind, love the arts (drawing, music, and/or drama) and believe that most of the significant ideas in life can't be expressed by talking or writing, which is all anyone seems to want to do in school. You have a hard time staying focused in most of your required classes. You are happy with yourself, but often feel like you are "marching to a different drummer."

Student 9

Who said academics and classes and grades are the most important things about school? As far as you are concerned, your classes are the places where you get to see your friends, and sometimes, frankly, classes seem to interrupt what's really important— like talking to your friends, and going to games, and participating in what they call the "extracurricular" activities. These activities don't seem "extra" to you at all, but instead are "central" to what school is *really* all about.

Group Building Activities

- ♦ Take an online Myers-Briggs test to indicate the personality type of each member.
- ♦ Read the book "Now Discover Your Strengths" by Marcus Buckingham and Donald Clifton. It comes with an online test to determine your top five strengths as well as your bottom two. Can go a long way in determining how to work with others.
- ♦ Descriptions of Team Building Exercises, Problem Solving Activities, & Initiative Games:
  - Blind Polygon
    [www.firststepstraining.com]
    Small group is blindfolded and given a length of rope, then asked to form various shapes with the rope e.g., a house.
  - Frenzy
    [www.firststepstraining.com]
    Game which seems to be competitive and impossible but can be solved via creative cooperation. Involves running and collecting balls.
  - Golf as a Team Building Exercise
    [F. John Rey, www.management.about.com]
    Group golf with nongolfers for teambuilding and exercise. Have at least two teams. Each person tees off. Next shots are played from the team's best shot.
  - Human Overhand
    [www.firststepstraining.com]
    Put lengths of rope between people. Task: tie a knot in the central piece of rope without letting go. Variation on Human Knot.
  - Limited Senses (Mute Line-up)
    [www.firststepstraining.com]
    People are blindfolded & given a unique number. Challenge is to line up in sequential order, without talking. Works on communication skills.
  - Newspaper Bridge Building
    [www.firststepstraining.com]
    A group constructs a bridge out of newspaper that has to be able to support a weight and allow passage of an object underneath.

- Quick Draw
  [www.firststepstraining.com]
  In 30 seconds, individuals try to circle as many sequential numbers on a worksheet as possible, then work as a group to solve. There is a secret pattern.
- Talisman
  [www.firststepstraining.com]
  A group is required to cross a 50 yd. distance. To cross, one must carry a talisman, and one can only carry the talisman once each way. Solution requires some people to carry other people.
- Traffic Jam
  [mathforum.org]
  Logic exercise which can be presented as a physical task. Gets groups thinking, sharing ideas, discussing, trialing solutions, and solving problems.
- Welded Ankle
  [www.firststepstraining.com]
  A group attempts to cross a distance with each person's feet "welded" to another person's feet.

Bloom's Key Words

Knowledge	choose, define, find, how, identify, label, list, locate, name, omit, recall, recognize, select, show, spell, tell, what, when, where, which, who, why
Comprehension	add, compare, describe, distinguish, explain, express, extend, illustrate, outline, paraphrase, relate, rephrase, summarize, translate, understand
Application	answer, apply, build, choose, conduct, construct, demonstrate, develop, experiment with, illustrate, interview, make use of, model, organize, plan, present, produce, respond, solve
Analysis	analyze, assumption, categorize, classify, compare and contrast, conclusion, deduce, discover, dissect, distinguish, edit, examine, explain, function, infer, inspect, motive, reason, test for, validate
Synthesis	build, change, combine, compile, compose, construct, create, design, develop, discuss, estimate, formulate, hypothesize, imagine, integrate, invent, make up, modify, originate, organize, plan, predict, propose, rearrange, revise, suppose, theorize
Evaluation	appraise, assess, award, conclude, criticize, debate, defend, determine, disprove, evaluate, give opinion, interpret, justify, judge, influence, prioritize, prove, recommend, support, verify

Taxonomy Table

Analyze the content standards looking at the verb and determining the level of the grade-level indicator.

Description of Standard	Knowledge	Comprehension	Application	Analysis	Synthesis	Evaluate

Tally Sheet for Standards and the State Assessment

District/School _____

Subject _____   Grade Level _____

Standard	Number of Times Found on State Assessment

Pacing Chart (Four-Part)

District _____

Subject Area _____

Grade Level _____

Grading Period 1 Standards	Grading Period 2 Standards	Grading Period 3 Standards	Grading Period 4 Standards

Hope List

District/School _____

Subject _____ Grade Level _____

What are 5 skills you hope every student graduating from this school has with regard to your subject area?

1.

2.

3.

4.

5.

Power Standards
"What–How–Who–When" Chart

District/School _____

Subject _____ Grade Level _____

Problem: How can you make sure that all relevant personnel are aware of the Power Standards?

What? What is your strategy?	*How?* How will you "roll out" the strategy?	*Who?* Who will be responsible?	*When?* When will it be finished?

Questions Conversion Chart

You can use the released tests found on your state's department of education website to determine the number and types of questions on your state assessment.
(It is recommended that you use two of the tests for your subject area to make sure the average is consistent, but this is not necessary.)

Total number of total questions
on the state assessment   _____ carry # down through this column

$$\downarrow$$

Number of multiple choice
questions   _____ ÷ _____ × 20 = _____ questions

$$\downarrow$$

Number of constructed
response questions (____ pts.)   _____ ÷ _____ × 20 = _____ questions

$$\downarrow$$

Number of constructed
response questions (____ pts.)   _____ ÷ _____ × 20 = _____ questions

$$\downarrow$$

Number of constructed
response questions (____ pts.)   _____ ÷ _____ × 20 = _____ questions

$$\downarrow$$

Number of response grid
questions   _____ ÷ _____ × 20 = _____ questions

$$\downarrow$$

Number of written responses   _____ ÷ _____ × 20 = _____ questions

Standard to Question Activity

Place the standard here:

Change the standard to a single question with the addition of only a few words:

Now break the question into a two, three, or four part constructed response depending on what format your state assessment follows:

Part A:

Part B:

Part C:

Part D:

Now try turning it into a multiple-choice question:

a.

b.

c.

d.

Assessment Analysis Worksheet

Analyze each question on your assessment and fill out the chart below indicating the question, the standard, the question format (multiple choice, constructed response [including points worth], or response grid), and the level of the question according to Bloom's Taxonomy.

Ques.	Standard	MC	CR	RG	PW	Lower Level Ques.			Higher Level Ques.		
						Know.	Comp.	Appl.	Anal.	Synth.	Eval.
1.											
2.											
3.											
4.											
5.											
6.											
7.											
8.											
9.											
10.											
11.											
12.											
13.											
14.											
15.											
16.											
17.											
18.											
19.											
20.											
21.											
22.											
23.											
24.											
25.											
26.											
27.											
28.											
29.											
30.											
TOTALS											

Assessment Checklist

Go over the assessment carefully. Use the checklist below to determine if the assessment meets the criteria.

Yes	No	
❏	❏	The type font is a good size for your students.
❏	❏	The format is acceptable: There is enough space for the answers, there are enough lines for the written answers, the lines are big enough with enough room in between them, there are not too many questions on each page, etc.
❏	❏	Each question is very clear. If the question is worth 2 points, the question clearly asks for 2 answers. If the question is worth 4 points, it clearly asks for a detailed answer.
❏	❏	The multiple choice questions have answers that are similar and require the student to think. There are no "off the wall" answers that the student can eliminate. The questions involve more than just recalling facts; the students need to be able to think, apply knowledge, and analyze information. There are at least 50% higher level questions.
❏	❏	The Directions for Administration and the Answer Key are not ambiguous, but are very clear. There are no "Accept Reasonable Answers." Specific examples are given for acceptable answers. When necessary, examples of unacceptable answers are given.
❏	❏	One point is given for each skill. Multiple points are not given for one skill. Ex: Instead of 3 pts. for 3 addition problems, 1 pt. will be given for 3 addition problems.
❏	❏	The levels of the questions match your Taxonomy Table.
❏	❏	There is a good distribution of multiple choice and constructed response questions that matches the state assessment.

Pacing Chart Confirmation

Take a look at the Academic Content Standards/Grade Level Indicators that you have placed in the designated column on your Pacing Chart. Write those standards on the chart below and check off whether or not they are assessed on this assessment.

Standard	Assessed on this Assessment	Not Assessed on this Assessment

Look at the standards that you have indicated are not assessed on this assessment. How will each of these indicators be assessed?

Writing Assessment Checklist

District/School _____   Date _____

Grade Level _____   Assessment # _____

Yes   No

❑   ❑   Assessment contains one writing prompt.

❑   ❑   Writing prompt covers the writing standards for your state.

❑   ❑   Assessment contains ratio of multiple-choice questions covered on the state assessment.

❑   ❑   Assessment contains questions addressing all the Content Standards for the designated quarter of the Pacing Chart.

❑   ❑   Assessment contains a Pre-Writing Section that the students will use prior to writing.

❑   ❑   Reading selections are grade appropriate.

❑   ❑   State Test vocabulary is used throughout the assessment.

❑   ❑   Assessment is formatted like the state test.

❑   ❑   Standards are identified for each item.

❑   ❑   Test administration (teacher directions) has been standardized.

❑   ❑   Scoring has been standardized: The writing prompts will be scored using a ____-point holistic applications scale and a ____-point holistic conventions scale. Application scores are double-weighted after scoring; convention scores are not weighted and are added to the total prompt. Multiple-choice items are scored as 1-point questions.

Reading Assessment Checklist

District/School _____ Date _____

Grade Level _____ Assessment # _____

Yes	No	
❏	❏	Assessment contains a fiction piece.
❏	❏	Assessment contains a nonfiction piece.
❏	❏	Assessment contains a poem.
❏	❏	Assessment contains questions addressing all the Content Standards for the designated quarter of the Pacing Chart.
❏	❏	Assessment contains the appropriate number of multiple- choice questions.
❏	❏	Assessment contains the appropriate number of constructed response questions.
❏	❏	Assessment contains 5–6 questions per selection. Assessment contains 15–30 questions.
❏	❏	Assessment contains higher level thinking questions (at least half of the questions).
❏	❏	Reading selections are grade appropriate.
❏	❏	State Test vocabulary is used throughout the assessment.
❏	❏	Assessment is formatted like the State Test.
❏	❏	Assessment contains charts and graphic organizers.
❏	❏	Content Standards are identified for each question.
❏	❏	Test administration (teacher directions) has been standardized.
❏	❏	Scoring has been standardized (pt. values, specific answers have been given, etc.).

General Assessment Checklist

District/School _____   Date _____

Grade Level _____   Assessment # _____

Yes	No	
❏	❏	Assessment contains questions addressing all the Content Standards for the designated quarter on the Pacing Chart.
❏	❏	Assessment contains appropriate number of multiple choice questions.
❏	❏	Assessment contains appropriate number of constructed response questions.
❏	❏	Assessment contains 15–30 questions.
❏	❏	Assessment contains higher level thinking questions (at least half of the questions).
❏	❏	Reading level is grade appropriate.
❏	❏	State Test vocabulary is used throughout the assessment.
❏	❏	Assessment is formatted like the State Test.
❏	❏	Assessment contains charts and graphic organizers.
❏	❏	Content Standards are identified for each question.
❏	❏	Test administration (teacher directions) has been standardized.
❏	❏	Scoring has been standardized (pt. values, specific answers have been given, etc.).

Directions for Short-Cycle Assessment

Test # _____   Estimated Time: _____

Materials needed:

1. Pass out the short-cycle assessment to each student and instruct them to write their names in the space provided. Distribute No. 2 pencils to the students who need them.

2. Say to the students:

   You are now going to start your short-cycle assessment for (subject) _____. Please turn to the beginning of your assessment. (Pause.) In this session, you will answer ____ questions. Some of the questions may be hard for you to answer, but it is important that you do your best. If you are not sure of the answer to a question, you should make your best guess. Do not mark your answers in the Question Booklet. Instead, mark your answers for this session in your Student Answer Booklet. Choose the best answer for each multiple-choice question and plan your written answers so they fit only in the answer spaces in your Student Answer Booklet.

   Only what you write in the answer spaces in your Student Answer Booklet will be scored. Some questions have more than one part. Try to answer all of the parts. If you are asked to explain or show how you know, be sure to do so. Does anyone have any questions? (Answer any questions the students have about the directions.)

3. Say to the students:

   It will probably take you about ____ minutes to answer the questions in this session of the test, but you can have more time if you need it.

   When you are finished with all the questions you may review your answers to the questions.

   If you get stuck on a word, I can read the word to you. I cannot read numbers, mathematics symbols, or a whole question to you. If you want help reading a word, raise your hand. (Pronounce the word to students who asked for assistance. Do not define the word or help the students in any other way.)

Are there any questions? (Answer any questions the students have about the directions.) **When you finish, please sit quietly and read until everyone is finished. You may begin.**

Directions to Read to the Student

Today you will be taking the Short-Cycle Assessment Test. This is a test of how well you understand the material we have covered over the last grading period.

Different types of questions appear on this test: multiple-choice, constructed response, and _____ (choose and add any that apply to your state)

All of your answers must be marked or written on your answer sheet.

There are several important things to remember:

1. You may look at any part of the test as often as necessary.
2. Read each question carefully. Think about what is being asked. If a graph or other diagram goes with the question, read it carefully to help you answer the question. Then choose or write the answer that you think is best on your answer sheet.
3. When you are asked to draw or write your answers, draw or write them neatly and clearly in the box provided.
4. When you are asked to select the answer, make sure you fill in the circle next to the answer on your answer sheet. Mark only one answer.
5. If you do not know the answer to a question, skip it and go on. If you have time, remember to return and complete the question.
6. If you finish the test early, you may check over your work. When you are finished and your test booklet and answer sheet have been collected, sit quietly until the time is up. (Other choices may appear here, such as "take out your silent work," etc.)
7. Write or mark your answers directly on your answer sheet. You may not use scratch paper. Use your test sheet to work out problems.
8. You may use the calculator that is provided, if applicable.

Anchoring Examples for Constructed Responses

Read the article "Brainy Birds" (http://www.mdk12.org/share/assessment_items/resources/brainy_birds.html) and answer the following question.

What other title would show the main idea of this article? Explain how your title would show the main idea. In your response, use information from the article that supports your explanation.

Sample Student Response #1

I think one other good title could be "Problem Solvers" because it sounds like ravens solve hundreds of problems almost every single day.

Annotation: The student identifies an appropriate title "Problem solvers" which indicates understanding of the main idea. The student states that "ravens solve hundreds of problems" but does not provide any details from the article to support this. There are several examples evident in the text that could have been used to support the title suggested by the student. For example, "if they can't find one kind of favorite food, they learn to eat something else."

Sample Student Response #2

Another title could be "Smart birds." That could be because ravens are very smart because they can copy sounds and even human speech.

Annotation: The student identifies a reasonable title, "Smart birds," but the word "smart" is merely a synonym for the word "brainy." This title could have been generated without reading the article. The student attempts to use information from the article, "copy sounds and even human speech," to support the title; however, this is a misreading of the article. A careful reader would discover that the article actually contradicts this statement by saying, "Copying sounds may not be a sign of smarts. . . ." The article does contain many points of information which when developed could add support to the response. For example, the article points out that "Ravens play more than most other birds," "have excellent memories," and "have a large brain." Any of these points, when developed by the student, would show a greater understanding of the main idea of the article.

Sample Student Response #3

Another title would be "A Ravens Brain" because it tells what a raven can do and how smart an raven is they tell sounds ravens can make and how heavy it's brain is. It can also swing by its beak of feet and it cans ride like a roller coastar in the air. It sad in the text that and ravens bran is 1/5 larger than an chickens brain.

Annotation: The student suggests a title for the article, "A Raven's Brain." This title looks like a good title at first; however, it does not relate to a main idea of the entire article which is more about aspects of ravens' behavior than about the characteristics of a raven's brain. In an effort to support the title, the student selects details from the article that relate specifically to the brain: "how heavy it's brain is" and that the " . . . ravens brain is ⅕ larger than a chickens brain." The student also includes some additional information from the article perhaps to lengthen the response, but this information is irrelevant.

Read the article "Adventure's Call" (http://www.mdk12.org/share/assessment_items/ resources/adventures_call.html) and answer the following question.

Explain how Jack London's experiences contributed to his career. In your response, use information from the article that supports your explanation.

Sample Student Response #1

Jack London's experences didn't only contribute to his correct it started it. For example his experience on the boat caused him to win the contest wich started his interest in writing. Then his experience in Yukon caused hom his first selling book. This also caused him to see the eror in the way we wrote. This is why I think his experences are his career

Annotation: The student identifies how London's experiences contributed to his career, and more importantly states " . . . it started it." The student accurately cites events and their contributions to London's career but does not fully explain the experiences and how they contributed. For example, the student could have explained that London's experience on the boat, his running into a typhoon, was used in his essay to win the contest.

Sample Student Response #2

Jack London's experiences have contributed to his career. Because he's writing about things that have happened to him and people he knows. Like when he was at the Klondike gold rush he's telling about what happened while he was there and it also tells how he sailed through a tycoon.

Annotation: The student states that London's experiences did help his career and refers in a general way to people and events that contributed to his writing. For example, the student refers to the Klondike Gold Rush but does not relate details from this event, such as his experience with Buck, the dog, which was later used by London in his novel.

Sample Student Response #3

Jack London's experiences contributed
to his career by . . . by giving him
something to write about. Like the
Klondike gold rush & how it changed his
life; and how when he was 17 years old he
went on a seal hunting expedition for
the coast of Japan.

Annotation: The student states that London's experiences contributed to his career and refers in a general way to these experiences. For example, the student identifies London's experience on "the Klondike gold rush and how it changed his life"; however, the student is not specific about how London's life changed. The student also references London's experience on a seal hunt, but a critical reader would explain the connection between the seal hunt and the start of London's writing career.

Directions for Student Profile Graph

How to use:

♦ Insert the student names in the provided space at the bottom of the graph.
♦ Draw a vertical line for the percentage score for each student, coloring it in to create a bar graph.
♦ Use a black marker and draw a horizontal line at the level that you consider proficient. (Many use a 75% line; however, you can choose to make that higher or lower.)
♦ Use a purple marker and draw a horizontal line at the percentage that is your class average. To calculate the class average, add all of the percentages together, and divide that number by the number of students who took the assessment. Now, compare the black line and the purple line. This shows the passage rate that you want to achieve and the actual passage rate of your class.
♦ Use a blue marker and draw a horizontal line at the percentage that is your upper curve line. To calculate this you need to find the standard deviation. To find the standard deviation you take each student's score and subtract it from the mean. For example, if the student scores are

$$64, 32, 56, 89, 91, 55$$

and the mean is 65, then you would subtract:

$$64 - 65 = -1$$
$$32 - 65 = -33$$
$$56 - 65 = -9$$
$$89 - 65 = +24$$
$$91 - 65 = +26$$
$$55 - 65 = -10$$

Next, you square each deficiency:

$$-1 \times -1 = 1$$
$$-33 \times -33 = 1089$$
$$-9 \times -9 = 81$$
$$+24 \times +24 = 576$$
$$+26 \times +26 = 676$$
$$-10 \times -10 = 100$$

Next, take these squares and add them together. It will look like this:

$$
\begin{array}{r}
1 \\
1089 \\
81 \\
576 \\
676 \\
+ \quad 100 \\
\hline
2523
\end{array}
$$

Now, divide that sum by the number of scores minus 1. So looking at our work above, that would be 2523 divided by 5 which equals 505.

◆ The last thing you will do is take the square root of this number. That is the standard deviation. In this case the square root of 505 is 22. If you draw a blue line 22 points above your mean of 65 then your upper curve line is 87.

◆ Use a red marker and draw a horizontal line at the percentage that is your lower curve line. To calculate this use your standard deviation from your upper curve line, which in the case above was 22, and draw your blue line 22 points below the mean of 65 which would place it on 43. Once you have your upper and lower curve lines using a standard deviation of 1, you should understand that statistically speaking, approximately 68% of your students will fall within the upper and lower curve. Any scores outside of this band, whether above or below, are considered to be statistically different than the rest of the scores. This is where you would look to remediate or enrich. Also, look at the number of students who are clustered right around the 75% line. These are your "bubble" students.

Student Profile Graph

Teacher _____ Grade Level _____ Assessment _____

100%																														
95%																														
90%																														
85%																														
80%																														
75%																														
70%																														
65%																														
60%																														
55%																														
50%																														
45%																														
40%																														
35%																														
30%																														
25%																														
20%																														
15%																														
10%																														
5%																														
Student's Name																														

Directions for Item Analysis Graph

How to use:

♦ Indicate the question number, along with the standard at the bottom of the graph along the y axis, and the percentages 0–100 on the x axis.
♦ Score the possible points for a particular question.
  • In other words, if you have 25 students taking the assessment and the question is worth 1 point, there are 25 possible points.
  • Similarly, if there are 25 students and the question is worth 4 points, possible points would be 25 × 4 = 100 points.
♦ Indicate the actual points the class earned.
  • In other words if 21 of the 25 students got the 1 point question correct, it is 21 actual points.
♦ To get the % mastered, divide the number of actual points divided by possible points.
  • 21 ÷ 25 = .84 or 84%
♦ Color in the bar graph according to the percent mastered.

This will give you an indication of how the class performed overall on each question, as well as classroom successes and gaps.

Blank Item Analysis

Teacher _____ Grade Level _____ Assessment _____

Question #	11	12	13	14	15	16	17	18	19	10	11	12	13	14	15	16	17	18	19	20	21	22	23	24	25
Standard																									
100%																									
50%																									
0%																									
Actual points																									
Possible points																										
% mastered																										

Directions for Non-Mastery Report

How to use:

- Go through each question and write what standard that question assessed in the blank provided using the coding from the Pacing Chart.
  - Example: Question 1, Standard: M 2-5
- In the lines provided, you may write out the standard for a reference to what the standard was covering. You may want to write the standard out word for word, or you may want to write a 1–2 word descriptor of it.
  - Example: Analyze problem situations involving measurement concepts, select appropriate strategies, and use an organized approach to solve narrative and increasingly complex problems.
- In the box provided, write all the names of the students in your class who did not master that particular question.
  - Example: Analyze problems. Remember, mastery for a constructed response question means the student scores a 75% or above.
    - Example: 3 points out of 4 is mastery
    - 2 points out of 4 is non-mastery
    - Example: 2 points out of 2 is mastery
    - 1 point out of 2 is non-mastery
- Go through all the questions placing the names of the students who did not master the question in the appropriate box.
- This list will give you an indication of how you can group students in your class if you need to go back and reteach a standard. This will also inform you which standard(s) you will need to reteach to the entire class, or if you need to go further into depth on a certain standard.

Non-Mastery Report

Question # _____ , Standard _____

_____

_____

_____

[ ]

Question # _____ , Standard _____

_____

_____

_____

[ ]

Question # _____ , Standard _____

_____

_____

_____

[ ]

Individual Assessment Reflection
(to be completed before attending the PLC meeting)

The students were most successful with which standard? (Item Analysis Graph)	
The students had the most difficulty with which standard? (Item Analysis Graph)	
Describe the questions the students had the most success with: multiple choice, constructed response, lower level, higher level, etc. (Short-cycle assessment)	
Describe the questions the students had the most difficulty with: multiple choice, constructed response, lower level, higher level, etc. (Short-cycle assessment)	
Looking at individual students, were there capable students who did not do well? Please list them. Implications? (Student Profile Graph)	
Looking at individual students, were there less capable students who did better than you thought they would? Please list them. Implications? (Student Profile Graph)	
Were you satisfied overall with your classroom performance on this assessment? Explain. (Student Profile Graph)	
Were you satisfied overall with your Grade Level performance on this assessment? Explain. (All Student Profile Graphs)	
Compare your class bar graph with the other class's bar graphs (if applicable). Comments? (All Student Profile Graphs)	
After reviewing the results, are there areas/types of questions/standards that you think need to be differentiated? What are they?	
What specific implications do you see for instruction during the next grading period? What will you do differently to change the results of the next assessment?	

Group Data Analysis for Assessment 1

Based upon data gathered regarding student performance on short-cycle assessments

5 _Most_ Successful Test Items from Assessment				5 _Least_ Successful Test Items from Assessment			
Item #	Standard	Specific Level of Bloom's	Kind of Question	Item #	Standard	Specific Level of Bloom's	Kind of Question

Instructional Implications: (Please list. Be as specific as possible.)

Once you have completed the analysis, check to be sure none of the least successful questions were a result of a question that was not clear or is not written to your satisfaction. If that is the case, make the revisions to the assessment.

Group Data Analysis for Assessment 2

Based upon data gathered regarding student performance on short-cycle assessments.

Most Successful Test Items from Assessment				*Least* Successful Test Items from Assessment			
Item #	Standard	Specific Level of Bloom's	Kind of Question	Item #	Standard	Specific Level of Bloom's	Kind of Question

How much time (approximate) was spent on instructing each successful item? On each of the least successful items? What is the relationship between the instruction time and the performance on the indicator?

What are the performance trends regarding the thinking skill level of the questions? How did the thinking skill level impact student performance?

Goals: Establish three instructional goals based upon the data you have analyzed for the next 9 weeks.

Strategies: For each goal, how will you implement strategies to achieve them?

Group Data Analysis for Assessment 3

Based upon data gathered regarding student performance on short-cycle assessments

5 _Most_ Successful Test Items from Assessment				5 _Least_ Successful Test Items from Assessment			
Item #	Standard	Specific Level of Bloom's	Kind of Question	Item #	Standard	Specific Level of Bloom's	Kind of Question

What changes in your instruction have caused students to improve their scores this year?

What are some future instructional implications? (Be as specific as possible.)

What are three goals you could set for the final assessment?

    1.

    2.

    3.

Group Data Analysis for Assessment 4

Based upon data gathered regarding student performance on short-cycle assessments

Most Successful Test Items from Assessment				Least Successful Test Items from Assessment			
Item #	Standard	Specific Level of Bloom's	Kind of Question	Item #	Standard	Specific Level of Bloom's	Kind of Question

Look at the results of Assessment 4 for your grade level. Do any of the data confirm the qualitative data represented in the "Hope List" activity? Please explain.
Are there specific standards that you feel the students have completely mastered based on the data? What are they?
Are there specific standards that you feel the students have **not** mastered based on the data? What are they?
What is one thing you would let next year's teacher know with regard to instruction based on your data? Please explain in detail.

Learning Style Inventory

Directions: Read each statement below and circle whether the statement applies to you seldom, sometimes, or often.

1. I like to write things down or to take notes for visual review.

   Seldom (0)   Sometimes (1)   Often (2)

2. I require explanations of diagrams, graphs, or visual directions.

   Seldom (0)   Sometimes (1)   Often (2)

3. I enjoy working with my hands or making things.

   Seldom (0)   Sometimes (1)   Often (2)

4. I am skillful with and enjoy developing and making graphs and charts.

   Seldom (0)   Sometimes (1)   Often (2)

5. I remember best by writing things down several times.

   Seldom (0)   Sometimes (1)   Often (2)

6. I can understand and follow directions on maps

   Seldom (0)   Sometimes (1)   Often (2)

7. I learn to spell better by repeating the words aloud than by writing the word on paper.

   Seldom (0)   Sometimes (1)   Often (2)

8. I can better understand a news article by reading about it in the paper than by listening to the radio.

   Seldom (0)   Sometimes (1)   Often (2)

9. I chew gum, smoke, or snack during studies.

   Seldom (0)   Sometimes (1)   Often (2)

10. I feel the best way to remember something is to picture it in your head.

    Seldom (0)   Sometimes (1)   Often (2)

11. I learn spelling by tracing the letters with my fingers.

    Seldom (0)   Sometimes (1)   Often (2)

12. I would rather listen to a good lecture or speech than read about the same material in a textbook.

    Seldom (0)   Sometimes (1)   Often (2)

13. I play with objects in my hands during learning period.

    Seldom (0)   Sometimes (1)   Often (2)

14. I remember more by listening to the news on the radio rather than reading about it in the newspaper.

    Seldom (0)   Sometimes (1)   Often (2)

15. I follow oral directions better than written ones.

    Seldom (0)   Sometimes (1)   Often (2)

A. Now add up the numbers for questions 2, 7, 12, 14, 15 and place the sum here: _____

B. Add up the numbers for questions 1, 4, 6, 8, 10 and place the sum here: _____

C. Next add up the numbers for questions 3, 5, 9, 11, 13 and place the sum here: _____

If your largest total is in group A, then you are an **Auditory** learner.
If your largest total is in group B, then you are a **Visual** learner.
If your largest total is in group C, then you are a **Tactile** learner.

Which type of learner are you? _____

If you are an AUDITORY learner, you remember what you hear and you enjoy class discussions. You also remember oral directions. For learning, you may wish to use tapes. Tape lectures to help you fill in the gaps in your notes. But do listen and take notes, reviewing notes frequently. Sit in the lecture hall or classroom where you can hear well. After you have read something, summarize it, and recite it aloud.

If you are a VISUAL learner, you remember what you see, and you enjoy visual projects and presentations. For learning, be sure that you look at all study materials. Use charts, maps, filmstrips, notes, and flashcards. Practice visualizing or picturing words/concepts in your head. Write out everything for frequent and quick visual review.

If you are a TACTILE learner, you remember what you experience with your hands or your body and you enjoy using tools or active lessons. You remember procedures after having done them. For learning, trace words as you are saying them. Facts that must be learned should be written several times. Keep a supply of scratch paper for this purpose. Taking and keeping lecture notes will be very important. Make study sheets.

Short-Cycle Assessment Performance Causal Checklist

Teacher _____   Date _____

Grade Level _____   Assessment # _____

Use the following checklist as you try to determine the cause of certain trends in the data from your short-cycle assessment. For the best analysis, this checklist should be completed within the Professional Learning Community.

Trend	Possible Cause	Yes	No
Certain students are low performing.	The students are on IEPs.	❑	❑
	The accommodations/modifications on the IEP were not followed.	❑	❑
	The IEP may need to be revisited.	❑	❑
Certain students are low performing	The students may need to be tested for learning problems.	❑	❑
	The students may have difficulty with writing skills.	❑	❑
	There may have been specific issues on testing day—not feeling well, being upset about something, etc.	❑	❑
	The students need to be taught within their learning style.	❑	❑
High performing students did not score as well as expected.	These students have good work on study skills—homework and class work completion, etc.—thereby leading to higher grades in class.	❑	❑
	These students may have had attendance issues during the grading period for this assessment.	❑	❑
	There may be specific issues—not feeling well, home problems—that may lead to lower achievement on the assessment.	❑	❑
Low performing students scored better than expected.	These students do not do homework regularly, thereby leading to lower grades in class.	❑	❑
	These students display behavioral problems, thereby leading to lower grades in class.	❑	❑
	These students do not complete class work, thereby leading to lower grades in class.	❑	❑
	These students have attendance issues, thereby leading to lower grades in class.	❑	❑

Trend	Possible Cause	Yes	No
Students did not do well on items assessing specific standards.	Not enough time was spent teaching the standard.	❑	❑
	Varying methods of instruction were not used in teaching these standards.	❑	❑
	The standard was not taught at the level at which it is written.	❑	❑
	Formative assessment did not occur along the way, thereby differentiated instruction did not occur.	❑	❑
	The question is unfair and needs to be rewritten.	❑	❑
Students did not do well on items in specific formats, e.g., short answer and extended response.	Students were not taught how to answer these types of questions.	❑	❑
	There was not enough practice in the classroom answering these types of questions.	❑	❑
	Formative assessment did not occur along the way regarding these types of items, so intervention was not provided.	❑	❑
	The question is unfair and needs to be rewritten.	❑	❑
Students did not do well on the questions requiring higher level, critical thinking. The class mean for the assessment was low.	Students are not taught and assessed at the higher levels on a consistent basis.	❑	❑
	The students were not taught the content necessary to enable them to be successful on this assessment.	❑	❑
	Some of the standards on the Pacing Chart were not taught because of time constraints.	❑	❑
	Students were not given exposure to the assessment format in class work and on unit tests.	❑	❑
Students do well at the beginning of the assessment, but fade out at the end.	Students are not provided practice answering multiple choice and constructed response questions on longer assessments throughout the grading period.	❑	❑

Any of the possible causes on which you checked "yes" are the ones that you need to pay attention to. You may need to do further analysis, revisions of the assessment, or make changes instructionally to reverse the trends.

Post-Assessment Revision Form

Teacher _____   Date _____

Subject _____   Assessment # _____

Complete this chart following administration of the assessment. This chart should be completed prior to the data analysis as far as listing the issues and possible revisions. Then, following the data analysis, the last column of the chart should be completed. This chart should be used when revising the assessment prior to the next administration.

Item #	Standard	Issue	Possible Revision	Complete Revision? Yes No
				❑ ❑
				❑ ❑
				❑ ❑
				❑ ❑

Item #	Standard	Issue	Possible Revision	Complete Revision? Yes No
				❑ ❑
				❑ ❑
				❑ ❑
				❑ ❑
				❑ ❑

Differentiated Instruction Flexible Groups

Examine your data. Decide on your flexible groups. Write the student's names for each group in the chart below, then detail how you will differentiate instruction to maximize achievement.

Flexible Group (Student Names)	Skill	Differentiated Strategy

Flexible Group (Student Names)	Skill	Differentiated Strategy

Student Questionnaire

1. Did you find the assessment easy? Why or why not?

2. What did you think about the testing schedule?

3. Did you think the classroom set-up made it easier or more difficult to concentrate on your assessment?

4. What did you think of the constructive response questions?

5. What did you think of your teachers' attitudes toward the assessment? Were they encouraging?

6. Did you feel prepared to take the assessment? Did your teachers teach the material you saw on it?

7. Were there any distractions that you feel could have been avoided?

8. What could be done to make your testing experience more comfortable?

9. What is your overall attitude toward assessments? Why do you think this is?

10. Did you try as hard on this assessment as you do your regular schoolwork? Explain why?

Observation Planning and Reflection Tool

Teacher _____

Subject _____ Grade Level _____

Fill out the following chart to document your schedule for observing your colleagues. This chart should be reviewed within the Profession Learning Community.

Type of Observation	Teacher Observed	Subject Area/Grade Level Observed	Date/Time of Observation
Classroom of Similar Subject Area			
Classroom of Similar Grade Level			
Classroom of neither subject area or grade level			

Reflections of Observation: _____

_____

_____

_____

_____

_____

_____

_____

Master Observation Schedule

Teacher Observing	Teacher Being Observed	Date	Time

Best Practice Sharing Chart

Listen as your colleagues share their best practices with the group. Record your questions for the persons sharing as they are presenting. Then, as a group or individually, reflect on ways that you might implement this best practice into your teaching.

Name of Person Sharing	Best Practice Shared	Questions	Reflections How I might use this in my classroom

Meeting Schedule

Meeting	Type/Length of Meeting	Topic
1		
2		
3		
4		
5		
6		
7		
8		
9		
10		

References

Barton, L. (1997). *Quick flip questions for critical thinking.* Dana Point, CA: Edupress.

DuFour, R., DuFour, R., & Eaker, R.(2005). *On common ground: The power of professional learning communities.* Bloomington, IN: Solution Tree (formerly National Educational Service).

DuFour, R., DuFour, R., Eaker, R., & Karhanek, G. (2004). *Whatever it takes: How professional learning communities respond when kids don't learn.* Bloomington, IN: Solution Tree (formerly National Educational Service).

DuFour, R., & Eaker, R. (1998). *Professional learning communities at work: Best practices for enhancing student achievement.* Bloomington, IN: Solution Tree (formerly National Educational Service).

Lang, S., Stanley, T., & Moore, B. (2008). *Short-cycle assessment: Improving student achievement through formative assessment.* Larchmont, NY: Eye on Education.

Marzano, R. (2003) *What works in schools: Translating research into action.* Alexandria, VA: Association of Supervision and Curriculum Development.

Moore, B., & Stanley, T., (2009). *Critical thinking and formative assessment: Increasing the rigor in your classroom.* Larchmont, NY: Eye on Education.

National school reform faculty resource book 2007–2008. Bloomington, IN: Harmony Education Center. http://www.nsrfharmony.org/resource_books.html

Stiggins, R., Arter, J., Chappuis, J. & Chappuis, S. (2006). *Classroom assessment for student learning.* Portland, OR: Educational Testing Service.

Tomlinson, C. & Allan, S. (2001). *How to differentiate instruction in mixed-ability classroom.* Alexandria, VA: Association of Supervision and Curriculum Development.

Wiggins, G., & Irua, L. (1997). *Educative assessment: Designing assessments to inform and improve student performance.* Jossey-Bass Inc.

Wiggins, G., & McTighe, J., (1998). *Understanding by design.* Alexandria, VA: Association of Supervision and Curriculum Development.

Wiggins, G. (1998). A true test. Toward more authentic and equitable assessment. *Phi Delta Kappan, 70.*